A Dictionary of British Institutions

D0512847

This book contains, in dictionary form, a selection of basic institutional terms and references which are widely employed in contemporary British life. Containing over 1400 short definitions, the book supplies instant and easy access in one volume to a wide variety of commonly used terms and phrases. The institutional terms are applied in a broad sense to cover, for example, political and governmental institutions; local government; legal, economic and industrial institutions; education; the media; religion and social welfare; health and housing institutions; social institutions and leisure and transport. The entries are alphabetically arranged and are accompanied by a glossary of abbreviations.

This guide is a succinct and simple reference tool that will be invaluable for students and teachers concerned with fundamental aspects of British civilization and society.

John Oakland is Senior Lecturer in English at the University of Trondheim, Norway. He is the author of *British Civilization: An Introduction*.

045791

A Dictionary of British Institutions
A student's guide

John Oakland

London and New York

First published in 1993
by Routledge
11 New Fetter Lane, London EC4P 4EE

Simultaneously published in the USA and Canada
by Routledge
29 West 35th Street, New York, NY 10001

Set in 10/12pt Times, Linotron 300 by Intype, London
Printed in Great Britain by TJ Press (Padstow) Ltd, Cornwall

Printed on acid free paper

British Library Cataloguing in Publication Data
A catalogue record for this book is available from the British Library.

Library of Congress Cataloging in Publication Data
Oakland, John.
A dictionary of British institutions: a student's guide/John Oakland.
p. cm.
Includes bibliographical references and index.
1. Great Britain–Civilization–Dictionaries. 2. Great Britain–
Social life and customs–Dictionaries.
DA110.O254 1993 92–38180
941'.003–dc20 CIP

ISBN 0–415–07109–7 (hbk)
ISBN 0–415–07110–0 (pbk)

Contents

Preface and acknowledgements

This book contains a selection of basic terms and references which illustrate some central institutional aspects of British national life. They reflect established values and practices, and are frequently used in contemporary Britain.

They are arranged alphabetically and cover agriculture, the arts, commerce, communications, education, employment, finance, geography, government, housing, industry, law, London, the media, medicine, the military, politics, religion, royalty, science, society, sport and leisure, and transport.

The book attempts to give students (particularly those from overseas) a short but informative insight into these terms, which may prompt a deeper and more detailed investigation of things British.

A book of this type necessarily draws many of its facts from a wide range of reference sources, too numerous to mention individually but to which a general acknowledgement is made. Particular thanks are due to *Britain: An Official Handbook* (London: HMSO), the current edition of which contains the latest information; *The Cambridge Illustrated Dictionary of British Heritage* (Cambridge: Cambridge University Press, 1986) edited by Alan Isaacs and Jennifer Monk; and Adrian Room, *An A to Z of British Life* (Oxford: Oxford University Press, 1990).

A

Abdication (royalty)
The constitutional procedure when a reigning monarch (king or queen) formally gives up the throne so that a younger member of the royal family can succeed, or because there is some obstacle to the monarch continuing to reign such as ill-health or incapacity. Edward VIII was the last British monarch to abdicate (1936), doing so because he wished to marry a divorced person.

Absolute discharge (law)
See **Penal system**.

Academic (education)
The term refers to a teacher in higher education (an academic), and also to the type of teaching and research which is carried on at this level. Such work is often distinguished from more vocational, fact-based or practical training.

Academic (school) year, the (education)
The year starts in late August/September for schools and in October for institutions of higher education, and ends in June for the latter and mid-July for the former. It is normally divided into three terms (or semesters in certain higher education sectors) and finishes for some pupils/students with examinations in the schools like the GCSE and A-levels, and with the finals of a first degree in higher education. It is distinguished from a calendar year which runs from 1 January until 31 December, and an income tax year (6 April to the following 5 April).

Access courses (education)
Special educational programmes usually in colleges of further education which provide a preparation for, and an appropriate test before enrolment on, a course of higher education for prospective students who do not possess the normal entry requirements. Such courses are designed to promote wider participation in higher education, especially for mature students and members of the ethnic communities in Britain.

Account (finance)
Either a current (non-saving) or a deposit (saving) arrangement

which an individual has with a bank or other financial institution (such as a building society). Some current accounts do not earn interest but deposit accounts invariably do.

Accused (the) (law)
A person who is charged with an offence under the criminal law, and who is referred to as the accused (or sometimes the defendant) at a subsequent trial.

Acquittal (law)
The court decision when a person is found not guilty (and therefore acquitted) of a criminal charge at the end of a trial. He or she is then free to leave the court, and in some cases may claim the costs which have been incurred in the proceedings.

Act (of Parliament) (government and law)
A statute or law (starting out as a bill) which has successfully passed through the three legislative bodies of Parliament (the House of Commons, the House of Lords, and formally the monarch by the Royal Assent), and represents the law of the land in a particular area. An Act is superior to any other form of law, except certain European Community law, and cannot be challenged in the law courts or by any other body on its merits (or content), except in some cases by the European Court of Justice (ECJ).

Adjournment (law and government)
A procedure, which can be employed in many contexts, whereby a meeting or hearing is postponed to a later time. For example, an adjournment of a court case may be over lunch, overnight or longer, and it may also be used in Parliament to postpone a particular sitting in both Houses or an item of business.

Administrative inquiries (law and government)
Official state bodies, consisting of an independent chairman and assessors, which are set up by government on an occasional basis to examine matters of public interest and concern, such as the proposed siting of nuclear power stations, coal mines, roads and airports. They are open to the general public and are also known as public inquiries. A report on the hearing and its conclusions will be sent to the relevant government minister who will then make a decision, but who need not implement the findings of the inquiry.

Administrative tribunals (law)
Official bodies which operate locally outside the ordinary system of the law courts and have judicial functions and independent assessors

who decide a wide range of civil cases. They are usually more accessible, less formal and less expensive than the conventional courts. They perform an important role in many areas of society, deciding disputes between private citizens (such as employment, and arguments between landlord and tenant); between public authorities and individuals (such as tax matters and social security); and in other areas such as immigration and discrimination (sex and race) cases.

Adoption (politics and law)
1. The procedure whereby a prospective Member of Parliament for a particular parliamentary constituency is chosen, after competition with other applicants, by a local constituency political party at an adoption meeting to be the official party candidate at the next general election or by-election. 2. The legal procedure whereby a childless couple applies to an adoption agency (such as the Church of England Children's Society) to have a child delivered into their custody and control. They then become the adoptive parents of, and are responsible for, the child.

Adult education (education)
An educational programme followed by a person who has already left secondary school at 16, either to obtain an academic qualification like the GCSE, or for recreational purposes. Adult educational courses, which are wholly or partly fee-paying, are normally provided by local government, colleges or voluntary groups on a weekly basis in school buildings, colleges of further education or community centres in the evening or at the weekend.

Advertising revenue (media and commerce)
The finance that is raised by commercial companies and media institutions (such as newspapers and independent radio and television) when they sell advertisements through their products and on their programmes. Such income is a very important part of many media institutions' total revenue.

Advertising Standards Authority, the (ASA) (media and commerce)
An independent organization that scrutinizes standards of advertising in the media and commerce on behalf of the general public and business interests. It applies the British Code of Advertising Practice, and evaluates whether advertisements are truthful, lawful or offensive. Complaints may be made to the ASA about specific advertisements, and the authority can advise that the advertisements be altered or removed.

Advisory, Conciliation and Arbitration Service, the (ACAS)
(employment and industry)
ACAS is an independent, government-financed organization, established in 1975. It consists of independent members and representatives from both sides of industry and may provide, if requested, advice, conciliation and arbitration services for the parties (usually employers and employees) involved in a dispute in both the public and the private sectors of the national economy. ACAS attempts to avoid or end strikes and industrial problems, and advises generally on industrial relations and employment matters.

Advocate (law)
The title of a lawyer in Scotland, similar to a barrister in England and Wales, who appears and speaks in court on behalf of clients. Sometimes used for a court lawyer, whether solicitor or barrister, in England and Wales, particularly in the case of solicitor-advocates.

Age of consent, the (law)
For legal purposes, the minimum age (currently 16) at which an individual may consent to and have sexual intercourse in heterosexual relationships only. In homosexual relationships the legal limit is 21 between consenting adults in private, although the law may be changed to reduce it to 18.

Age of criminal responsibility, the (law)
Children in Britain under the age of 10 cannot be held responsible in law for their criminal actions, but those between 10 and 14 may be held responsible depending on the circumstances. Children between 10 and 17, who are properly accused of a criminal offence, are tried in special children's courts, known as youth (formerly juvenile) courts in England and Wales, children's panels in Scotland, and juvenile courts in Northern Ireland.

Albert Hall (Royal), the (arts and London)
A large public hall in central London, constructed between 1867 and 1871, which is a forum for important national functions. The hall holds a range of concerts (such as the annual Promenade Concerts), parades, meetings, religious services (like the Royal British Legion Remembrance service), ceremonial occasions, light entertainment and sporting events.

A-level (Advanced level) GCE, the (education)
The highest academic school examination (General Certificate of Education), normally taken at the age of 17 or 18 in the sixth form

of secondary schools in England and Wales, two years after the lower GCSE examination. It is the essential qualification for entrance to higher education and to most forms of professional training, and pupils will normally sit the examination in three subjects.

Alien (society and law)
A person living in Britain who is neither a British citizen as of right nor a naturalized British citizen. It is often used to refer to foreigners in general or non-Britons such as refugees and political asylum seekers.

Alliance Party, the (of Northern Ireland) (politics)
A small non-sectarian political party established in 1970 in response to the current problems in Northern Ireland, but with no representation in the House of Commons. It is mainly a middle-class party composed of Catholics and Protestants and advocates conciliatory and moderate policies in an attempt to reduce tension and bring the two communities closer together.

Amendment (government)
An agreed (or majority-voted) change or addition which is made to a legislative bill in its passage through Parliament. The alteration may be proposed by the government or the opposition parties, and in both Houses of Parliament. Amendments may be used in other contexts outside government.

Anglican (religion)
A member of the Church of England, but the term also refers to the larger Anglican Communion in Britain and overseas which has its origins in the Church of England. The various churches of the Communion have similar doctrines and forms of worship based on the Book of Common Prayer and the Thirty-Nine Articles of Belief. Their ruling structure is episcopal (by bishops) and they meet at periodical Lambeth Conferences in London under the chairmanship of the Archbishop of Canterbury.

Anglo-Catholic (religion)
A member of the Church of England who is sympathetic to some of the religious doctrines and practices of the Roman Catholic Church, and sees ritual, the authority of the clergy and observance of the sacraments as important elements of religion. Anglo-Catholics generally belong to the High Church wing of the Church of England.

Anglo-Irish Agreement, the (government)
A governmental agreement reached in 1985 between the United
Kingdom and the Republic of Ireland which attempts to secure
greater security and political stability in Northern Ireland, and advocates a power-sharing arrangement between Catholics and Protestants in the province as an initial step to resolving problems there.
The republic has for the first time been brought into direct and
frequent talks with the British government on the Northern Irish
situation.

Annual percentage rate, the (APR) (finance)
The percentage amount of total annual interest, after including all
other interest rates in a particular transaction (such as a monthly
interest rate), which is charged by a finance company when it lends
money to an individual or organization in a loan arrangement.

Appeal (law)
The legal procedure whereby a person (the appellant), who has
been found guilty of a criminal offence and sentenced, may appeal
in certain circumstances against the conviction and/or the sentence
to a higher court. In England and Wales, the appeal is usually
heard either by the crown court (from the magistrates' court) or
by the Court of Appeal (Criminal Division) from the crown court.
The ultimate court of appeal is the House of Lords. Appeals may
also be made in civil cases to the High Court, the Court of Appeal
(Civil Division) and the House of Lords. National appeal courts
are used in Scotland and Northern Ireland at the intermediate
levels, and the House of Lords may be involved at some of the
higher levels. Further appeals may be made to the European Commission of Human Rights and the European Court of Justice (ECJ).

Appellant, the (law)
See **Appeal**.

Apprentice (employment)
A young person who prepares for a particular trade, such as that
of bricklayer, plumber or electrician, by a period of practical training over a specified number of years (an apprenticeship). The
person will gain experience and knowledge by helping and working
with a qualified craftsman. It is also necessary in some trades to
pass written and practical examinations.

Arbitration (employment and law)
The method used in an employment or business dispute between

parties, such as a strike or partnership disagreement, to resolve the situation, with an independent person or body (such as ACAS) acting as an intermediary or arbitrator.

Archbishop of Canterbury, the (religion)
The religious leader and spokesman of the Church of England. He is known officially as the Primate of All England, denoting responsibility for the whole Church in England.

Archbishop of Westminster, the (religion)
The religious head of the Roman Catholic diocese of Westminster in London and often regarded as the spokesman for the Roman Catholic Church in England and Wales, who also has the title of Cardinal granted by the Pope. Roman Catholic archbishops in Scotland and Ireland perform a similar role.

Archbishop of York, the (religion)
The deputy religious leader of the Church of England. He is known officially as the Primate of England denoting responsibility for the northern section (or province) of the Church in England.

Archdeacon (religion)
A senior clergyman and administrator in the Church of England, normally based in a cathedral and to whom the bishop delegates a range of duties, which may be both administrative and religious, at the cathedral and in the diocese generally.

Areas of outstanding natural beauty (AONBs) (geography)
The 39 rural areas in England and Wales designated by the Countryside Commission of England (CC) and the Countryside Council for Wales (CCW) which are similar to national parks, but which do not have public services in them. They are protected by parliamentary legislation (such as the Town and Country Planning Act 1971), and development in them is restricted. Similar bodies and areas exist in Scotland and Northern Ireland.

Aristocracy (society)
A historical, but still common, term to describe those people belonging to a section of the upper class in Britain. The senior aristocracy are the peers (dukes, marquesses, earls, viscounts and barons), also known as the nobility, while the minor aristocracy, also known as the gentry, are people such as knights and others with inferior titles.

Armistice Day (society)
The day (also known as Poppy Day) that officially marks the ending

of the First World War on 11 November 1918. On the nearest
Sunday to this date every year, Remembrance Sunday commemorates the memory of the dead of the two world wars and later
conflicts, with people wearing artificial poppies made by the Royal
British Legion (RBL), symbolizing the real flowers from the corn-
fields of Flanders in the First World War. Parades and services are
held throughout Britain, including those at the Cenotaph.

Army, the (military)
Control of the British Army is vested in the civilian government,
although the monarch formally remains commander-in-chief of all
the armed forces. Army personnel increased in the two world wars
due to military conscription or compulsory national service (which
ended in 1957). The army currently consists of professional volunteers with a total of some 147,000 men and women, who can serve
for short or long terms, although substantial cuts are now being
made because of events in eastern Europe since 1989.

A-road (transport)
A main road (sometimes known as a trunk road), which is not a
motorway, often connecting large towns and cities, and which carries lorries and heavy vehicles in addition to cars. All A-roads have
numbers, such as the A1 from London to Edinburgh and the A40
to South Wales. A(M)-roads are those larger A-roads which may
sometimes connect up directly to a motorway. B-roads are secondary or minor roads (also numbered) which often run across country
and connect A-roads and motorways.

Arrest (law)
The legal procedure when a person either actually committing, or
who is suspected of having committed, a crime is taken into custody,
usually by the police.

Articles (media and law)
1. Feature pieces of some length in newspapers and other printed
material which comment upon particular items (normally of topical
interest), and which are usually written by specialists. Leading articles often appear on the editorial page and are written either by
the editor or editorial staff. 2. For solicitors, the period of up to
two years when a student after passing professional examinations
has to undertake practical training, usually in a solicitors' firm,
before becoming a fully qualified lawyer.

Arts Council (of Great Britain), the (ACGB) (arts)
A government body created in 1946 to promote and support the

arts in Britain. Its government-appointed but independent members are responsible for awarding grants of government money to representatives of the subsidized arts, such as theatres, ballet and opera companies, art galleries and orchestras, in London and the provinces.

Ascot (sport and leisure)
A racecourse near Windsor, England, at which the annual Royal Ascot four-day horse-race meeting is held in June. It is attended by the royal family, and has the fashionable Ladies' Day on the second day.

Ash Wednesday (religion)
See **Lent**.

Ashes (the) (sport and leisure)
Refers to test matches (cricket competitions) played between England and Australia alternately in both countries, with the Ashes (or prize) being awarded to the winner of a series of matches. The term originated in 1882 when England were beaten for the first time by Australia in England. A mock obituary lamented the death and subsequent cremation of English cricket and the sending of the ashes to Australia. Later a cricket ball was actually burned and the ashes deposited in an urn. Today the urn is kept permanently at Lord's cricket ground in London, regarded as the home of world cricket.

AS-level (Advanced Supplementary Level), the (education)
An advanced school examination (supplementary to the A-level) which was introduced in 1988–9 in England and Wales. It was intended to increase the opportunities for those students who might lack the academic ability for, or do not want, the full A-level. The examination can be taken after one year's study as a separate subject, and some students may choose to take two full A-level and two AS-level subjects to qualify for entry to higher education and the professions.

Assault (law)
In the criminal law, an intentional use of violence to cause bodily harm to another person. One of the commonest offences in British criminal statistics.

Assembly (education and government)
1. In many schools (whether independent or state) the occasion when all children and teachers gather together (or assemble) for a

particular purpose, such as a religious service at the beginning of the school day. 2. In government the legislative body in which politicians could potentially gather to debate and decide policy. Power-sharing assemblies between Catholics and Protestants have been tried without success in Northern Ireland, and have also been proposed as devolved self-governing bodies for Wales and Scotland.

Assisted area (government and commerce)
An economically depressed region where the government encourages industrial development and job creation by offering special grants and financial loans to companies willing to establish themselves there. There are two kinds of assisted area: development areas mainly in central Scotland, north-east England, the Midlands and south-west Cornwall; and intermediate areas in the same regions, with a lower priority than development areas.

Assisted Places Scheme, the (education)
A policy introduced by the Conservative government from 1980 by which academically gifted children from low-income families may attend an independent school, and have some or all of their school fees paid for by the state, depending on parental income.

Association Football (soccer) (sport and leisure)
The officially correct term for football (or soccer), which is different from rugby football. It derives from the Football Association (FA) founded in 1863 which formulated the modern rules of the game and which, through its national associations in England, Wales, Scotland and Northern Ireland, controls amateur and professional football in Britain.

Astra (satellite), the (media)
The satellite (together with the Marcopolo satellite) from which British Sky Broadcasting (B-Sky-B) and cable television channels are transmitted to those British viewers who subscribe to the satellite and cable companies and who have a satellite-receiving dish or cable facilities. The Astra and Marcopolo satellites currently transmit some 11 channels in Britain.

Asylum (political) (law)
The refuge which may be given in Britain to a fugitive from another nation. Asylum is usually reserved for victims of political, religious or other discrimination, who fear a threat to life in their own countries, but the qualifications for acceptance are being tightened.

Attainment tests (education)
As part of the Conservative government's reforms of the state school system from 1988, attainment targets are being devised to establish what children should normally be expected to know, understand and do at the ages of 7, 11, 14 and 16. The progress of each child is to be measured against uniform standards under the new National Curriculum, and the results of the tests (carried out in individual schools by teachers) are to be made available to parents and others.

Attendance centre (law)
A local government institution which young criminal offenders (under 20) are sentenced by the court to attend for various forms of training and instruction instead of receiving a custodial sentence in a young offenders' institution. They may be sentenced to spend up to 24 hours at the centre, normally on Saturdays, and for a maximum of three hours on each occasion.

Attorney (law)
An individual, usually but not always a lawyer, appointed by a will or a person to act for that other person in business, property or legal transactions, particularly when that person is old, incapacitated, or otherwise incapable of managing his or her own affairs.

Attorney-General, the (AG) (law)
The senior law officer of the Crown and government in England and Wales who acts as the government's chief legal adviser and sometimes leads government prosecutions in court. He is usually an MP, a member of the Privy Council, and serves as the head of the bar. He is a political appointment of the sitting government, and is replaced on a change of government. The Lord Advocate in Scotland performs similar, but broader, functions.

Audience (government)
The weekly meeting at Buckingham Palace that the Prime Minister has with the monarch at which matters of state are discussed. This maintains the historical link between the government and the sovereign, and also allows the monarch to be informed of, as well as to comment on, government business.

Authorized Version, the (AV) (religion)
A well known English translation of the Bible written in 1611, 'authorized' (although not formally) by King James I, and

consequently also called the King James Bible. It is widely used in Anglican churches.

Automobile Association, the (AA) (transport)
One of the two main organizations for motorists, together with the Royal Automobile Club (RAC), which provides its members with advice, assistance in the event of breakdowns on the roads, legal aid, technical help and specialized services (such as insurance). It also publishes travel books and guides.

Average national income (finance and employment)
The gross annual figure (currently about £12,500) which represents the average income for an individual in Britain, calculated from all gross national wages and salaries. But there are substantial deviations above and below this norm.

B

Bachelor's degree (BA, BSc) (education)
A degree (Bachelor of Arts or Bachelor of Science), also known as a first degree, granted by institutions of higher education to a student who has successfully completed a programme of studies in arts or science (usually of three years' duration). At Oxford, Cambridge and some other universities the BA is a first degree in both non-science and science subjects.

Backbencher (government)
An elected Member of Parliament (MP) in the House of Commons who does not hold any government or Official Opposition office and who sits on the back benches, behind the front benches which are reserved for ministers on the government side and members of the Shadow Cabinet on the opposition side.

Back-to-back houses (housing)
A row of terraced houses which is physically joined at its rear to an adjoining row of similar houses. They are historically associated with the urban building programmes of the Industrial Revolution in the late eighteenth and the nineteenth centuries, which used all available space in the new industrial centres. Similar housing still exists today in the inner-city areas of some towns and cities.

Badminton Horse Trials, the (sport and leisure)
See **Eventing**.

Bail (law)
In criminal cases, the release by the magistrates' court under the rules of the Bail Act 1976 of an accused person awaiting trial. The person is then freed from custody, but may have to satisfy certain conditions of bail, such as reporting at specific times to a police station or surrendering a passport, prior to the eventual trial.

Bailiff (law)
An official in the courts service who delivers writs and summonses (to attend court) on individuals, makes arrests in certain situations, collects fines, and whose office generally implements court decisions.

Balance of payments, the (finance)
The relation between all national payments in and out of Britain over a given period (usually a month), based on the number of exports and imports, and resulting ideally in a balance (or even a profit). Sometimes, however, the result is a trade deficit (or gap) when exports do not compensate for imports.

Ballot (politics and industry)
The process whereby a (usually) secret written vote is taken on a particular item. This may be associated with politics (as at a general or local election) or in industrial relations matters (such as prior to an official strike), but can occur in other contexts.

Ballot paper (politics)
The sheet of paper on which a voter places his or her vote in a polling booth at a by-election, general election or local election, and which is then placed in the ballot box. The names of the candidates and their parties are printed on the ballot paper, and the voter marks 'X' against the name of the preferred candidate. A ballot paper may be used in other situations where a vote or an election is called for.

Bank holiday (society)
An official state or public holiday on a weekday (except Saturdays and Sundays) when most public facilities and offices, shops and factories are closed. The current bank holidays in England and Wales are New Year's Day (or the first weekday following it); Good Friday; Easter Monday; the first Monday in May (May Day Bank Holiday which may be abolished soon); the last Monday in May (Spring Bank Holiday); the last Monday in August (Summer Bank Holiday or August Bank Holiday); Christmas Day (or the Monday after it, if it is a Saturday or Sunday); and Boxing Day (or the next weekday after Christmas Day). There are some different bank holidays in Scotland (such as August Bank Holiday on the first Monday in August) and Northern Ireland.

Bank of England, the (BE) (finance)
The central national bank of England and Wales, situated in the City (of London), which was established in 1694 and nationalized in 1946 by the Labour government. It prints and circulates banknotes, acts as the government's financial adviser, decides the bank rate, implements government monetary policy and seeks to maintain stability in the financial markets, domestically and abroad.

Bank of Scotland, the (finance)
The second largest (after the Royal Bank of Scotland) and oldest (founded in 1694) of the leading Scottish banks. It prints banknotes which are used in Scotland, and generally acceptable in England and Wales.

Bank rate, the (finance)
The percentage amount of interest, based on prevailing national and international trends and within the restrictions of the European Exchange Rate Mechanism (ERM) if Britain rejoins, at which the Bank of England lends money to borrowers (mainly banks). This generally fixes the rate charged by other banks and financial institutions to their customers.

Bankruptcy (finance)
Legal proceedings to deal with the liabilities of an insolvent debtor or bankrupt (individual or company). Its purpose is to distribute the bankrupt's assets fairly among the creditors (people and groups owed money) and it attempts to free the bankrupt from further liability. Bankruptcy may be instituted by the debtor (voluntary) or by the creditors (involuntary).

Baptism (religion)
In most Christian Churches in Britain, baptism (or symbolic purification by water, often known as christening) is the sacrament required for formal membership of a Church. It is normally accomplished by sprinkling water on a person's head (often an infant), or sometimes by full immersion in water, as with the Baptists.

Baptists, the (religion)
A Protestant (non-Anglican) Christian Church originating from 1608, and one of the Free Churches in Britain. It has about 160,000 adult members (only adult members are baptized by full immersion in water). Most of the originally independent Baptist Churches are now members of the Baptist Union of Great Britain and Ireland (established in 1812–13), and there is a big Baptist membership in Wales.

Bar, the (law)
The name for the professional legal organization to which all barristers in England and Wales belong. The Bar Council (the General Council of the Bar) is the governing body of the Bar, regulates the activities of barristers and serves as a professional association or

trade union for them. There are similar organizations for similar lawyers in Scotland and Northern Ireland.

Barbican Centre, the (arts and London)
A large cultural complex in London which was completed in 1982 near the City (of London), and contains a wide range of amenities and services. Its theatre is the London base of the Royal Shakespeare Company, and the Barbican Hall is the home of the London Symphony Orchestra (LSO), a leading orchestra founded in 1904.

Barclays Bank (finance)
One of the five leading English banks, founded in 1896, with branches throughout Britain, providing banking and financial services to private customers and commercial companies.

Barrister (law)
In England and Wales, a lawyer who has been admitted to one of the Inns of Court and 'called to the Bar' as a full member of the legal profession. A barrister is self-employed, advising on legal problems usually provided by solicitors, and arguing cases in the higher criminal and civil courts, based on the brief (or documents on the case) supplied by a solicitor. In general, the public do not have direct access to a barrister but must proceed through a solicitor.

Base (lending) rate, the (finance)
The percentage amount of interest (such as 14 per cent) at which individual banks lend money to private and commercial borrowers, and which may vary between banks. Other financial institutions, such as building societies, often set their own interest rates by this figure. The base rate is governed by the Bank of England's bank rate.

Basic rate (finance)
The amount of income tax (at present 25 per cent) charged on an individual's taxable income up to £23,700, although the lowest bands are now subject to 20 per cent. A higher rate of 40 per cent is charged on incomes over £23,700.

Bath and West, the (agriculture)
See **Royal International Agricultural Show**.

Battle of the Boyne, the (politics)
See **Orangemen**.

BBC, the (British Broadcasting Corporation) (media)
One of the two leading radio and television broadcasting organizations (together with the ITC) in Britain, established in 1927, with
its headquarters at Broadcasting House in London. It operates
under a royal charter, which is reviewed by Parliament at periodic
intervals, but generally has an independent role in its policy-making
and programme-planning. It broadcasts domestically on local radio
stations throughout Britain, through the national radio stations of
Radios 1–5, and on the television channels of BBC 1 and 2. It also
provides radio and television broadcasts by the BBC World Service
at Bush House in London for listeners and viewers overseas.

BBC 1 (media)
The majority-viewing national television channel of the BBC,
broadcasting a wide range of programmes such as light entertainment, musical and variety shows, news, sports, current affairs,
children's television, drama productions, films and educational
series for some 20 hours daily.

BBC 2 (media)
The second (minority-viewing) national television channel of the
BBC, broadcasting generally, but not exclusively, programmes of a
more serious nature than those of BBC 1, such as Open University
courses, documentaries, drama, concerts and English-speaking and
foreign films for some 18 hours daily.

BBC World Service, the (media)
A broadcast service of English and 34 foreign-language radio programmes which is transmitted 24 hours a day to overseas countries
by the BBC from Bush House in London. It has now been extended
to a television service for cable and satellite subscribers worldwide.

Bear (finance)
A financial speculator on the (London) Stock Exchange who sells
shares anticipating that their price will fall and that a profit can
then be made by buying them back.

Beat, the (law)
The popular reference to a policeman regularly patrolling a local
neighbourhood on foot (walking the beat) or by bicycle. This form
of community policing has been largely replaced by car patrols, but
some police forces are increasingly returning to it.

Bed-and-breakfast (housing and commerce)
A common and relatively cheap service in Britain which provides

travellers and tourists with a bed overnight and breakfast the next morning usually in a small hotel, boarding house or private home.

Bedsitter (housing)
A small combined living unit, usually in a large house and rented out to one person, comprising a sitting-room/bedroom and some basic cooking and washing amenities.

Belfast (geography and government)
The capital of Northern Ireland situated on the country's east coast, and historically the centre of government and administration in the province. The city, with a population of over 300,000, is an important educational, commercial and heavy industry centre specializing in shipbuilding and aircraft construction, but currently suffering from high unemployment and violent civil disturbances.

Bench, the (law)
A collective term referring to the magistrates or judges in a British court of law, who in the past would sit on a raised bench to hear a case, and who are still seated above the main body of the court room.

Betting shop (sport and leisure)
The premises of a bookmaker who is specially licensed by a magistrates' court to accept bets or wagers (gambling) on such activities as horse- and greyhound-racing. Bookmakers also take bets in many other areas, such as the result of a general election or a sporting event.

Big Bang (finance)
The popular term for the substantial changes which were made in the organization of the London Stock Exchange in October 1986 under the Conservative government's policy of deregulation (freeing institutions from restrictions and regulations so that they might operate more competitively). Previously potential investors were required to buy and sell stocks and shares through a stockbroker, who traditionally operated on the Stock Exchange floor with a jobber (who set the prices of securities). Now those financial companies which are members of the Stock Exchange have become broker/dealers, and are permitted to trade directly both with investors and other companies. An integrated computer system at the Stock Exchange provides share prices and other information for dealers, who operate mostly by telephone from their corporate offices.

Big Ben (London and media)
The bell of the clock in the main tower (St David's Tower) of the
Houses of Parliament, London, which is used as a time signal by
the BBC and Independent Television News.

Bill (government)
The draft (or printed proposal) of an Act of Parliament, which
passes through five stages of debate, amendment and decision in
both Houses of Parliament (first reading, second reading, committee
stage, report stage and third reading), before receiving the Royal
Assent and becoming an Act of Parliament.

Bill of Rights (1689), the (government)
This bill marked a stage in the triumph of parliamentary rule over
royal power. It curtailed royal authority to suspend laws, maintain
an army, and raise money without the consent of Parliament. The
Bill of Rights is still regarded as one of the fundamental documents
of the British constitution and of British liberty.

Bishops (religion)
The senior clergy of those Christian Churches in Britain, such as
the Church of England and the Roman Catholic Church, which
have episcopal rule, or government by bishops. Many bishops are
based in ancient cathedral cities and are responsible for the administration of their individual dioceses. Twenty-four senior bishops of
the Church of England also sit in the House of Lords.

Black Rod (government)
An official of the House of Lords (formally called the Gentleman
Usher of the Black Rod but commonly known as Black Rod
because of the black stick that he carries during ceremonies) whose
chief functions are looking after security, accommodation and
services in the House. He also calls the members of the House of
Commons to attend the annual Royal Speech from the Throne in
the House of Lords at the opening of a new session of Parliament.

Block vote (employment and politics)
A voting system in which one delegate's vote at a conference or
election counts as the total number of votes cast by the organization
or group the delegate represents. This method is used by the Trades
Union Congress (TUC), and the Labour Party at its annual conference and party elections (although the system is being amended).

Blood donor (medicine)
An individual, in good health and aged 18–70, who volunteers some

of his or her blood for later use in blood transfusions in hospitals or elsewhere in emergency situations. The collection of blood is organized by the state Blood Transfusion Service, which establishes regional transfusion centres and arranges donor sessions as required in a variety of locations.

Blood sports (sport and leisure)
The hunting and killing of wild animals such as foxes, hares, deer and otters by hunts on horseback with dogs and by individuals on foot. This activity has been militantly opposed by the League Against Cruel Sports (founded in 1924) and other animal rights' groups which campaign for the abolition of all blood sports.

Blue chip (finance)
A share issued by reputable leading companies on the (London) Stock Exchange. It is seen as a secure low-risk investment which will give a good dividend (profit), and maintain its price in adverse economic conditions.

Blue-collar worker (employment and industry)
A skilled industrial worker (in contrast to a white-collar clerical worker), who traditionally has often worn blue overalls at work. Such workers have been increasingly associated with middle-class status in terms of home- and share-ownership, income and aspirations, and have recently supported the Conservative Party in increasing numbers.

Board (commerce)
A small group of directors who are responsible for and manage a commercial company. The term can also be used in connection with executive structures in governmental and educational institutions.

Boarding school (education)
Usually an independent primary or secondary school where pupils live during term time at the school rather than at home, and where they also receive their education. The boarding sector has decreased substantially in recent years.

Boat Race, the (sport and leisure)
An annual rowing race (the University Boat Race) between two teams (each one consisting of eight rowers and a cox) from Oxford and Cambridge Universities, first held in 1829. It takes place on a 4½-mile (7.2-km) stretch of the River Thames in London in March or April.

Bonfire Night (society)
See **Guy Fawkes' Night**.

Book of Common Prayer, the (BCP) (religion)
The officially approved prayer and service book of the Church of
England, originally printed in 1549, which regulates the form, content and order of religious worship in church services. Any proposed
changes in its composition have to be approved by Parliament.
Some churches now use a more contemporary version, the Alternative Service Book.

Bookmaker (sport and leisure)
A licensed individual who accepts bets of many different kinds from
the public, but particularly on horse- and greyhound-races, either
in a betting shop or at the actual races, and who pays out any
winnings. Colloquially known as a bookie, although the formal
name is a turf accountant.

Borough (government)
1. A local area in England outside London (a burgh in Scotland)
which is usually represented in the House of Commons by one MP.
Most boroughs are now in practice local government districts but
may have kept their ancient title. 2. One of the 32 administrative
districts into which London is divided for local government purposes, and which have taken over most of the functions of the
former Greater London Council (GLC).

Borough council (government)
A local government authority with elected councillors in a borough,
such as the 32 boroughs in London but also elsewhere in England.
Outside London it is principally responsible for small-scale local
services such as housing, sanitation, planning permission and rubbish collection, and implements the large-scale policy decisions of
the county council in whose area it is situated.

Bowls (sport and leisure)
A popular outdoor game for most age groups and both sexes (also
known as bowling), with teams of from two to eight players. Its
purpose is to gently roll a wooden ball (bowl) over a grass lawn
(bowling green) so that it stops as near to a small white ball (the
jack) as possible.

Boxing Day (society)
The day (26 December) after Christmas Day, and an official bank
holiday, on which homeowners earlier gave Christmas boxes

(presents or money) to servants and tradespeople. The tradition still continues with gifts (usually money) being distributed to regular visitors, such as rubbish collectors, the milkman/woman and paper-boys/girls.

Brass band (arts)
A group of players of brass musical instruments. Brass bands are popular as amateur entertainment throughout Britain, but especially in the north of England. They have distinctive identities and uniforms, take part in band contests, and draw their musicians from social and employment backgrounds such as factories, coal mines, religious or charitable groups, and schools.

Breakfast TV (media)
The common term for national early morning television (6.00 am–9.00 am), capable of reaching some 54.8 million viewers. The two breakfast television channels until 1993 were 'Breakfast News', broadcast by BBC 1, and 'Good Morning Britain', broadcast by TV-am of ITV, from Monday to Friday. TV-am lost its 1991 bid to continue the franchise, and was replaced in January 1993 by GMTV with a licence for 10 years on Channel 3. Both channels provide news bulletins and commentary, weather reports, sports features and interviews.

Brief (law)
See **Barrister**.

Britain (geography and politics)
A common short name for both Great Britain (England, Scotland and Wales) and the United Kingdom of Great Britain and Northern Ireland, employed equally as a political and geographical reference.

Britannia Royal Naval College, the (BRNC) (military)
A training and educational college for cadets who intend to become officers in the Royal Navy, first established on HMS *Britannia* in 1836, at Dartmouth, Devon, now known commonly as Dartmouth.

British Academy, the (BA) (arts and education)
An independent society established in 1901 to further studies mainly in the humanities. It elects distinguished academics to fellowships, and provides financial and academic aid to educational institutions and individuals in Britain and overseas.

British Airports Authority, the (BAA plc) (transport)
The private company that owns, operates and maintains seven of

the biggest and most important airports in Britain, such as Heathrow, Gatwick, Stansted (in England) and Prestwick (in Scotland). Most other airports are owned and controlled by local government authorities.

British Airways (plc), (BA) (transport)
The biggest British airline, which was established following various mergers of existing companies in 1974 as a state concern. It was privatized in 1987 and operates scheduled, charter and cargo services worldwide.

British Association, the (BA) (science)
An influential independent body (the British Association for the Advancement of Science) founded in 1831 to encourage a wide interest in science among scientists and the general public. It organizes lectures, exhibitions and publications, and holds an annual conference.

British Athletics Federation (BAF) (sport and leisure)
The governing body of men's and women's amateur athletics in Britain, which in 1991 replaced (among other national groups) the Amateur Athletics Association (AAA) founded in 1880 and the Women's AAA founded in 1922.

British Board of Film Classification, the (BBFC) (arts)
An influential independent organization established in 1912, to which all films intended for public viewing must be shown, and which grants an appropriate certificate or category for them: U certificate (general admission allowed), PG (admission under parental guidance), 12 (no child under 12), 15 (no child under 15) and 18 (no child under 18). It may refuse to grant a certificate to films considered unsuitable or insist that cuts be made.

British Coal (Corporation), the (BC) (government)
The state organization established in 1947 by the nationalization of the then private coal industry which operates Britain's coal mines. It is currently responsible for some 50 collieries or mines and employs some 44,000 miners principally in South Wales, Nottinghamshire, Derbyshire, South Yorkshire and West Yorkshire. British Coal has increased its productivity in recent years because of a large investment in improved technology. Some 83 per cent of the coal produced is currently used by power stations to generate electricity, and the rest goes to domestic and industrial users and

a small amount to exports. British Coal has been included in Conservative government privatization plans.

British Council, the (government)
A semi-independent cultural body (or quango), with its main headquarters in London, founded in 1934. It furthers a knowledge of Britain and the English language overseas, operates offices worldwide, and promotes educational and technical co-operation with other countries.

British Film Institute, the (BFI) (arts)
A national body, which is mainly government-financed, founded in 1933 to promote film-making in Britain and which has a substantial library of film and television material. It administers the National Film Theatre (NFT) in London, founded in 1951, which shows films on a daily basis, and holds an annual London Film Festival.

British Gas plc (science and commerce)
British Gas is a private company created by the privatization in 1986 of the previously state-run body, which had supervised the manufacture and distribution of gas in Britain. British Gas is now the main public supplier of North Sea gas, but acts as a common carrier for regional companies which supply gas through the company's transport network. The activities of the gas companies are monitored by the Office of Gas Supply (Ofgas) following privatization, and the Gas Consumers Council looks after the interests of consumers.

British Grand Prix, the (sport and leisure)
1. A major international motor-car racing championship (part of the World Championship) held at the Silverstone course in Northamptonshire (reputedly the fastest in the world). 2. A motor-cycle racing championship held annually at various circuits such as Silverstone and Donington Park, Leicestershire.

British Isles, the (geography)
A geographical (not political or constitutional) term for England, Scotland, Wales and Ireland (including the Republic of Ireland), together with all offshore islands.

British Library, the (BL) (arts)
The biggest public library in, and the national library of, Britain, consisting of several different libraries mainly in London. It is also a copyright library which means that it receives a free copy of all

books published each year in Britain. It has long suffered from lack of space and most of its library operations are being gradually transferred to a new building near St Pancras, London.

British Medical Association, the (BMA) (medicine)
The professional and disciplinary organization, established in 1832, that supports the interests of doctors and surgeons. It is the trade association (or union) for all general practitioners (GPs), and negotiates on their behalf with government. It also serves to publicize and promote medical and scientific knowledge.

British Movement, the (politics)
An extreme right-wing nationalist political party with aims similar to those of the National Front (NF), such as restrictive policies on immigration, the economy and the European Community (EC). It has little popular support and no representation in the House of Commons.

British Museum, the (BM) (arts)
A well known museum in London established in 1753 which holds extensive collections of antiquities and historical artefacts, and a famous Reading Room. It previously housed a large reference library which is gradually being transferred to the new British Library building.

British Nuclear Fuels (plc) (BNFL) (science)
A nuclear fuel organization owned by the British government. It provides services for the whole nuclear process, manufactures nuclear fuel and reprocesses nuclear waste (at Sellafield in the north-west of England). It has suffered from a negative public image in recent years because of radiation leaks and public concern about the safety of nuclear energy.

British Open Championship, the (sport and leisure)
The oldest major golf championship in the British Isles, established in 1860, which is played at different golf courses (such as St Andrews in Scotland) on a rotating basis.

British Rail (BR) (transport)
The state organization that supervises and operates Britain's railway system, except for Northern Ireland. It is divided into regions in Great Britain: Anglia, London Midland, Western, Southern, Eastern and Scottish. BR has been included in Conservative government privatization plans.

British Sky Broadcasting (B-Sky-B) (media)
An independent satellite television company which beams some 11
channels from the Astra and Marcopolo satellites to British homes
fitted with satellite-receiving dishes. It was formed by the merger
in 1990 between British Satellite Broadcasting and Sky Television
and individuals pay subscriptions for its services.

British Standards Institution, the (BSI) (science)
An independent body established in 1901 which works with government, commerce and industry to formulate acceptable standards,
safety criteria and testing methods for commercial and industrial
products and processes in Britain. Attempts are being made to
establish common European and international standards, particularly in terms of the working of the internal European market.

British Summer Time (BST) (society and communications)
The time of the year, normally from March to October, when
British clocks are set one hour ahead of Greenwich Mean Time
(GMT) so that maximum use may be made of the daylight. British
times are one hour behind western European norms for most of
the year.

British Telecom (BT) (communications)
The organization which was formerly part of the state-run Post
Office, but which was separated from it and eventually privatized
in 1984 as a public limited company (plc). It now operates the
majority of the telecommunications systems in Britain such as the
telephone network. The Office of Telecommunications (Oftel) is
the independent regulator of BT following privatization.

British Tourist Authority, the (BTA) (government)
The state organization created in 1969 which publicizes and promotes tourism in Great Britain (both domestically and abroad), and
liaises with the separate English, Scottish and Welsh national tourist
boards. The BTA publishes a monthly magazine *In Britain*, established in 1930, which contains information for overseas readers and
visitors to Britain.

British United Provident Association, the (BUPA) (medicine)
The largest British medical insurance company which organizes
payment for private medical treatment in private hospitals and
clinics, and in pay-beds in the National Health Service (NHS).
Subscribers pay insurance premiums to the company for such cover.

There are additional medical insurance schemes organized by other companies, such as Private Patients' Plan.

British Waterways (Board), the (BW/BWB) (government, sport and leisure)
The state-owned board is responsible for some 2,000 miles (3,200 km) of waterways (canals) in Great Britain. Canals were originally used for transporting freight throughout the country as part of an inland waterway network, which was largely constructed during the Industrial Revolution in the late eighteenth and the nineteenth centuries. They are still used for limited commercial and freight purposes, but also for boating and leisure activities and holidays.

B-road (transport)
See **A-road**.

Broadcasting Complaints Commission, the (media)
An independent body created in 1988 and financed by the BBC, ITC, the Radio Authority and S4C (the commercial Welsh-language channel in Wales). It evaluates complaints of unfair treatment in television and radio broadcasts and of any abuse of privacy in the preparation and presentation of programmes.

Broadcasting Standards Council, the (media)
The government-appointed council consists of independent members. It acts as a public watchdog over standards of taste and decency in television and radio programmes, and advertisements. It monitors programmes and evaluates complaints from the public, and its findings, under statutory powers, have to be published by the broadcasting organizations concerned.

Broadmoor (law and medicine)
A state psychiatric institution and special hospital (Broadmoor Hospital) founded in 1873 in Berkshire which treats mentally ill patients. It is better known for its secure residential section where severely disturbed people who have been convicted of criminal offences are kept. There are other similar special hospitals in Britain, whose existence is currently under review.

Broadsheet (media)
A term to describe the large-page format of the quality national newspapers, as opposed to the tabloid (or small-page) size of the popular newspapers.

Broker (finance)
An independent financial agent who buys and sells commodities or

services, such as insurance and shares, for another person and is paid or receives a commission for such work.

Brownie Guides, the (sport and leisure)
See **Guides Association**.

Buckingham Palace (royalty and London)
The official residence of the sovereign in central London, built in 1703, where the monarch lives for most of the year and from which much state and royal business is conducted. The ceremonial Changing of the Guard is held daily in its courtyard. The sovereign has other official residences (such as Windsor Castle) and private properties like Sandringham in Norfolk and Balmoral in Scotland.

Budget, the (government)
The proposals and plans itemized every year by the sitting government for public taxes and spending over the next financial year. The Chancellor of the Exchequer presents them to the House of Commons in a traditional speech (Budget Speech) in March or April, and the proposals have to be passed by Parliament in order to become law. Mini-budgets (or economic statements) may also be required during the course of the year. It is possible that budgets may be announced at different times, and in a different format, in future years.

Building societies (finance)
Private incorporated banking organizations (appearing under many different names throughout Britain) which were first established in the eighteenth century. They are now financed by investment deposits from members of the public on which interest is paid by the building society. Loans (or mortgages) are then made from this capital to people who wish to build or buy a house or flat. Building societies currently offer their depositors a wider range of banking and investment services than the traditional mortgage.

Bull (finance)
A financial speculator on the (London) Stock Market who buys shares, usually at the bottom of the market price, anticipating that their value will increase so that a profit can be made when they are eventually sold.

Bungalow (housing)
A one-storey house, where the living accommodation and other utilities are on the same (usually ground-floor) level. It is a common

housing alternative for people (such as the disabled and elderly) who do not want a two-or-more-storey property.

Burglary (law)
In England and Wales, the common offence of entering a building or home as a trespasser (a burglar) with intent to commit a crime, such as theft. If the offender possesses a weapon the offence is aggravated burglary. In Scotland, the equivalent offence is called housebreaking.

Burke's Peerage (society)
A well known reference work first published in 1826 and updated annually that provides alphabetically organized biographical information about the British peerage and aristocracy. A similar register of the peerage is *Debrett*, first issued in 1802.

Burns' Night (society)
An annual celebration held on 25 January in Scotland and by Scots worldwide, to commemorate the anniversary of the birth (1759) of Robert Burns, Scotland's national poet. The event often includes a supper at which traditional Scottish dishes (such as haggis) are eaten, a piper plays Scottish music, Burns's poems are read, toasts are drunk, and Scottish dancing may be performed.

By-election (politics)
A parliamentary election to elect a new MP, held in one constituency only, at any time between a previous general election and the next. This may be necessary because the sitting MP has retired or died, or been elevated to the House of Lords. Parliament as a whole is not dissolved.

Bye-law (law)
A law passed by a local authority such as a district council to regulate specific (and usually small-scale) services and activities in its area.

By-pass (transport)
A road or motorway which is built specifically to go round (by-pass) a town, city or village, so that through-traffic is diverted from these areas. This reduces traffic congestion, particularly in the inner cities, and the by-pass system (or circular roads) has been widely used in modern Britain.

C

Cabinet, the (government)
The small group of 20–4 government ministers who are largely (but not exclusively) the heads of the most important ministries or departments in Whitehall. They are appointed by the monarch on the recommendation of the Prime Minister to perform an executive role in collectively deciding (and often initiating) government policy, maintaining control of government and co-ordinating the work of government departments. The Cabinet normally meets once a week privately at No. 10 Downing Street (the Prime Minister's official London residence) when Parliament is in session. Although much of the Cabinet's work is done through cabinet and ad hoc committees, this centring of policy- and decision-making in a small group of people in Britain has traditionally been known as cabinet government.

Cable television (media)
Television pictures can be transmitted by means of signals through a cable (instead of broadcasting). The commercial possibilities of cable were not exploited in Britain until the late 1970s, and have progressed relatively slowly since then. The Cable Division of the ITC has since 1991 been responsible for issuing licences to cable companies, supervising their programmes and promoting cable development. Cable services are paid for by subscription.

Calendar year (society)
See **Academic (school) year**.

Call to the Bar (law)
The procedure by which a student barrister in England and Wales, after passing professional and academic examinations, is admitted to the Bar and becomes a full member of the profession.

Cambridge University (education)
One of the two oldest and best known universities in England (together with Oxford University). It has a collegiate structure, being composed of 28 independent colleges, such as King's, Trinity and St John's, the earliest of which were founded in the thirteenth century. Two colleges are for women only, while the rest are coedu-

cational. Currently some 10,000 students are in residence, of whom nearly half are women.

Campaign for Nuclear Disarmament, the (CND) (society)
An organization established in 1958 to campaign specifically for the abolition of nuclear weapons in Britain and worldwide. It also fights for the reduction of conventional military weapons and has a current membership in Britain of some 90,000.

Campus (education)
The name for the physical surroundings and buildings in which a British institution of higher education is situated, although traditionally the term has been more associated with universities.

Canon law, the (law and religion)
The law of the religious courts in Christian Churches, such as the Church of England and the Roman Catholic Church, which is based on ancient legislation and decisions derived from ecclesiastical councils and the senior hierarchy of the Churches. It once had an extensive social and legal importance, but today it deals only with religious matters.

Canterbury Cathedral (religion)
Canterbury in Kent became the ecclesiastical capital of England after St Augustine and other Roman monks had converted the pagan Saxons to Christianity in AD 596–7. The present cathedral was built between the eleventh and fifteenth centuries embodying the styles of several architectural periods, and became a centre for religious pilgrimages after the murder there of Archbishop Thomas Becket in 1170. It is the religious seat of the Archbishop of Canterbury.

Canvass/canvassing (politics)
The procedure at election time in Britain when local and national representatives of the political parties visit homes and other venues in a constituency trying to gain information about voting intentions, and attempting to persuade voters to vote for their party.

Capital Gains Tax (CGT) (finance)
A state tax levied at the relevant rate of income tax (currently 25 per cent or 40 per cent depending on levels of personal income) on profits of £6,000 or more which an individual or organization makes from the sale or disposal of assets, such as property, material objects or shares.

Capital punishment (law)
Historically in Britain, the execution by hanging of a criminal convicted of serious crimes such as murder, also known as the death penalty. The punishment was abolished in 1965, but may still legally be used for treason. It has been replaced by life imprisonment, which normally entails confinement in prison for a minimum of 21 years, although prisoners may be released before this time and some may be retained for longer.

Cardiff (geography)
The capital city of Wales on the south-east coast of the country, with a population of some 273,000. It is a leading industrial area and port, an administrative and commercial centre, and a university city.

Carol service (religion)
A Christian religious service which comprises modern and traditional Christmas carols (songs or hymns) and selections from the Bible about the birth of Christ. It takes place in the weeks prior to Christmas, usually in a church, chapel or cathedral, but also in the open air. Such services are widely popular and are frequently broadcast on television and radio.

Case law (law)
Another name for the English common law. It represents the decisions, originally oral but gradually written, taken by judges in actual court cases. Today the proceedings are published in official law reports such as the *All England Law Reports*.

Casting vote (society)
When the voting on a matter results in a tie (an equal number of votes), the chairperson is usually allowed to decide the issue by casting an extra vote (therefore having two votes).

Cathedral city (geography)
An ancient city with an old-established cathedral (usually of the Church of England), such as Lincoln, Durham, Salisbury and Winchester, which is normally the headquarters of a diocese. These cathedrals will often have a cathedral school attached to them, some of whose pupils sing in the cathedral choir. The title of city was often granted by the monarch because of the existence and religious importance of the cathedral.

Ceefax (media)
See **Teletext**.

Celtic (society and geography)
A term descriptive of those regions (and their people) of the United
Kingdom, such as Wales, Scotland, Cornwall and Northern Ireland,
whose populations are largely of Celtic origin, and where Celtic
languages (such as Gaelic) may still be spoken. Celtic invaders and
settlers came from Europe to these areas in the period from 600
BC to the first century AD.

Cenotaph, the (society)
A large stone memorial in Whitehall, London, built to the memory
of those who died in the First World War. An annual memorial
service is held here on Remembrance Sunday, with the laying of
wreaths to honour those who died in both world wars and later
conflicts, and a two-minute silence is observed at 11.00 am. The
sovereign, public and government figures, representatives of overseas countries, members of the armed services, and other groups
are usually present.

Census (government)
A periodic survey of the population or certain aspects of the activities of the country. The first modern British census was held in
1801 and then every 10 years since 1841 (except 1941). Censuses
are now conducted by the Office of Population and Censuses in
England and Wales and similar official bodies in Scotland and
Northern Ireland. Governments often make use of the demographic
information obtained, and any changes observed, to plan future
state policies.

Central Criminal Court, the (law)
The correct official name of the main criminal court in England, at
(and known popularly as) the Old Bailey, in East London. It is
now in practice a crown court centre.

Central government (government)
The term used to distinguish the activities of the central government
located in Parliament and Whitehall, London, from those of local
government areas throughout Britain. The term 'centralization'
often indicates how such authority is increased, while 'decentraliz-
ation' illustrates the reverse process of a movement away from
central to local government.

Central government grant (government and finance)
A sum of money (also known as a revenue grant) from public
income or taxation that is granted by central government to local

government authorities, which enables them to carry out and finance their functions and services. Some 70 per cent of local government income now comes from central government.

Central Office of Information, the (COI) (government)
A state body which prepares and publishes official government material and public information on a wide range of topics, both domestically in Britain and overseas.

Certificate of Pre-Vocational Education, the (CPVE) (education)
An intermediate school examination introduced in 1986 for pupils in England and Wales who choose to remain at school for an extra year after the age of 16 and after taking their GCSE examination. It is supposed to prepare them for employment or a vocational course, and ranks below the higher A-level and AS-level.

Chamber of commerce (commerce)
An independent body of businessmen, traders, shop owners and industrialists in a British town or city, which furthers and looks after business interests locally and nationally, and which is a member of the national Association of British Chambers of Commerce.

Chambers (law)
1. The room (or collection of rooms) where a barrister works and where he or she may interview clients and solicitors. In London, chambers are mainly situated in the Inns of Court, and outside London are located in special chambers buildings in a town or city.
2. A judge's room in a court building in which special or confidential cases are heard in private, and in which he or she may also hear minor cases. A registrar will have similar facilities in a local civil court.

Chancellor (education)
The nominal or formal head of a university (and sometimes of other institutions of higher education), who has no executive role. He or she holds the position for life but visits the institution only on special occasions, such as degree presentations and other ceremonies. However, the Chancellor may have an important role in cases where arbitration and appeal procedures are required.

Chancellor of the Exchequer, the (government)
The official title of the British finance minister, who is a senior member of the Cabinet and in charge of preparing the annual national Budget. As head of the Treasury (or the department con-

cerned with the national economy) the minister is responsible for government and state finances.

Chancery Division (of the High Court), the (law)
The branch of the High Court in England and Wales which deals with civil cases involving financial matters, property, wills and companies, as well as equity (the settlement of cases in a fair way).

Channel 3/ITV (media)
Under the Broadcasting Act 1990 the national independent ITV channel was renamed Channel 3 in January 1993 (also still called ITV). The new channel, which operates for some 24 hours daily, is made up of 15 regionally based licensees (or production companies) of the ITC, such as Central, Anglia and Yorkshire, and an additional ITC licence providing a national breakfast-time programme (granted to GMTV). The 10-year licences were awarded to the companies which bid successfully for the new franchises in 1991.

Channel 4 (media)
An independent national television channel of the ITC established in 1982. It is something of a minority channel when compared to the majority-viewing ITV (Channel 3) and broadcasts specialized documentaries, detailed news reports, films and plays for some 24 hours daily. It is also required by law to transmit programmes which appeal to minority groups in society. Channel 4 became a public corporation in 1993, selling its own advertising time and retaining the proceeds. S4C is its Welsh-language channel in Wales which is government-funded.

Channel 5 (media)
A new national independent television channel, supervised by the ITC, which is to be established by 1994. Due to limited frequency availability it will cover only about 75 per cent of households in Britain. A 10-year franchise (licence) will be awarded to the successful bidding company, and the new channel will be financed through advertising, subscription or sponsorship, or a combination of these.

Channel Islands, the (geography and government)
See **Crown dependency**.

Channel Tunnel, the (transport)
The rail tunnel constructed by an Anglo-French private company under the English Channel between England and France and designed to carry vehicles and passengers on specially constructed trains.

Chapel (religion)
1. A small place of worship with its own altar in a cathedral or large church, which is set apart from the main body of the building. 2. A separate building or place of worship in an institution such as a college, school or hospital. 3. A Nonconformist (non-Anglican) religious building.

Charities (society)
Charities are voluntary organizations which provide services over a wide range of activities like education (such as a public school) and social welfare. They are largely dependent upon public donations or fees, although some may obtain local government grants. Their charitable status means that any income they receive is not subject to tax. There are 171,000 charities and other voluntary organizations in Britain, such as Oxfam, Shelter, the Royal Dispensary for Sick Animals and the Church of England Children's Society, which perform valuable and important functions. The Charity Commission is the government organization that supervises all registered charities.

Chequers (government)
The house in Buckinghamshire that is the official country residence of the Prime Minister, and where government and international meetings may be held.

Chief Constable (law)
The senior police officer who is in operational command of one of the 52 police force areas in Britain, and who has organizational, managerial and disciplinary responsibility for the police officers in the area.

Chief executive (government)
In local government, the principal professional official who is in charge of the bureaucracy or administration of a district or county council. He or she is not elected and functions similarly to a civil servant.

Child benefit (finance)
A weekly state benefit within the social security system paid to a mother for all the children in a family (usually up to the age of 16). The present amount is £10.00 for the eldest child and £8.10 for each additional child. Single-parent families are given an additional sum for the first or only child.

Children's panel (law)
See **Age of criminal responsibility**.

Christie's (commerce)
A leading firm of auctioneers in London founded in 1766, which buys and sells a range of antiques but specializes in fine art, and at whose auctions world-record prices are achieved.

Christmas (religion and society)
An important religious festival for Christians in Britain, which celebrates the birth of Christ. For most Britons it is a family holiday season, and focuses on Christmas Day (25 December) with its Christmas dinner. Presents and greetings cards are given, a Christmas tree (usually a fir tree) is erected and decorated, and parties, pantomimes and carol services are held. The Christmas season traditionally starts on Christmas Eve (24 December), and lasts until Twelfth Night (6 January) when decorations are taken down.

Church of England, the (C of E) (religion)
The established Christian Church in England was founded as a national Church by the Act of Supremacy 1534, after which it developed from a Roman Catholic into a Protestant Church. The sovereign is the secular head of the Church; its religious leader is the Archbishop of Canterbury; and its senior ruling hierarchy of archbishops, bishops (24 of whom sit in the House of Lords) and deans are formally appointed by the monarch on the advice of the Prime Minister. The Church is not completely free of state influence since its forms of worship are subject to approval by Parliament, although it receives very little state finance. A government-appointed body (the Church Commissioners) manages its considerable finances and property holdings, and a General Synod acts as the governing body of the Church in religious and organizational matters. The active membership of the Church is some 2.2 million, but many more people have been baptized or confirmed in the Church.

Church of Scotland, the (religion)
The national Presbyterian Church in Scotland, created in 1560 by John Knox. It is independent of state control, it organizes its own spiritual and doctrinal affairs, and its ministers and members have complete equality. Individual churches are democratically organized by a kirk session, comprising the minister and elected members (elders) of the church, and a General Assembly under the leadership of an elected Moderator serves as a national governing body. The current adult membership of the Church is about 838,000.

Citizens' Advice Bureau, the (CAB) (society)
A voluntary body with branches in most towns and cities throughout Britain. It supplies information to the public on a range of matters, and gives specific advice about civil rights, legal problems, state benefits and voluntary aid resources.

Citizen's arrest (law)
A British citizen has an ancient, if largely unused, right to arrest any person who is actually committing, or is suspected of having committed, certain serious crimes (such as those which are punishable by imprisonment).

Citizens' Charter (government and society)
A programme introduced by the Conservative government in 1991 which, by promoting greater openness and providing more information, is intended to improve standards of service for the consumer and give specific rights to members of the public in their relations with state businesses, such as education, health, the Post Office, transport and employment. The scheme is being expanded to a range of other fields.

City (geography)
The official title of most large towns in Britain, which has historically been granted by the monarch. This may have earlier been due to the town's religious significance as a cathedral centre, but later the title was often awarded because of special achievements or economic importance.

City (of London), the (London and government)
An independent local government area in East London, with its own police force and institutional structures. It is one of the world's main financial and commercial centres, and its territory of one square mile or 2.6 sq. km (the Square Mile) comprises banks, the Bank of England, the Stock Exchange, legal firms and many financial and insurance companies.

City technology college (CTC) (education)
State colleges for secondary-level pupils, with an emphasis on science, business and technology, established by the Conservative government and private business since 1988 in selected urban areas. The colleges are state-aided but independent of local education authorities (LEAs).

Civic Trust, the (CT) (society)
A voluntary organization established in 1957 which has a network

of local trusts in England, Scotland and Wales. It preserves and maintains ancient monuments, historic buildings and the environment, usually in urban centres.

Civil Aviation Authority, the (CAA) (transport)
An independent body that monitors and regulates the activities of British airlines and airports, and provides navigation functions, air traffic control systems and safety facilities in the skies over Britain.

Civil courts (law)
Those courts of law which apply the civil (as opposed to the criminal) law. The lowest in England, Wales and Northern Ireland is the county court, followed by the High Court of Justice, and the Court of Appeal (Civil Division). Scotland has a similar structure but with different names.

Civil law (law)
That branch of the law which deals with property, commerce and companies, wills and succession, the family, contracts and non-criminal wrongful acts done by one person to another, as well as constitutional, administrative and industrial matters. It attempts to settle disputes between people, and between individuals and organizations.

Civil List, the (royalty and government)
A sum of money, now frozen at 1990 levels for a period of 10 years, granted out of state funds and approved by Parliament, which is made to the sovereign and the immediate members of the royal family to cover the expense of their public duties.

Civil servant (government)
A civilian career administrator employed by the Civil Service, who impartially serves the current government in London and throughout the country, and implements the policies of that government. He or she remains in the job despite a change of government, but there are restrictions on political activities and publication in order to preserve the neutrality of the service.

Civil Service, the (government)
The state administrative organization or bureaucracy which consists of ministries or departments mainly in London (Whitehall), but with agencies and branches in other parts of the country. It is staffed by professional civil servants and is responsible for implementing the policies of the current government at all levels of national life.

Clan (society)
Members of an extended family group, mainly in Scotland but also in Ireland, who have a common ancestor and (normally) the same surname (such as Campbell and Macdonald). The hereditary head of a clan is normally called a chieftain or chief.

Clearing bank (finance)
British banks have a central clearing house system in London whose membership consists of individual clearing banks such as the main English and Scottish national banks. It acts as the central organizer for the daily transfer and exchange of finance and cheques between the various banks by settling all accounts itself for its members.

Clerk of the House of Commons, the (government)
An administrative official employed by the House of Commons. He or she has a central role in the House, advising the Speaker on Commons procedure and being present at all sittings of the House.

Clerk of works, the (government)
Usually a professional official in local government, who monitors council building work and is responsible for the maintenance and repair of a wide range of council property, such as parks, recreation grounds and school buildings.

Clerk to the Justices, the (law)
The professionally qualified lawyer in a magistrates' court who advises the magistrates on points of law and procedure, but who cannot influence or interfere with their decisions. He or she also grants legal aid to applicants.

Closed shop (employment, commerce and industry)
In the past all the workers in most factories or other places of employment had to join an officially recognized trade union. Non-trade union workers or unionists belonging to non-recognized unions were not employed. Conservative government legislation since 1979 has now eased the situation by prohibiting the compulsory membership of a trade union.

Closing price, the (finance)
The final daily price of stocks and shares recorded at the end of trading on the (London) Stock Exchange, which remains fixed until business starts again the next day.

Club (society)
A regulated association (usually owning club premises) whose mem-

bers have common interests such as sport, politics, hobbies or employment. There is a wide range of clubs in Britain covering the social spectrum from working men's clubs to prestigious London clubs.

Coalition (politics and government)
A joint government (relatively rare in Britain) comprising different political parties. This may happen in wartime, or when no one party has an overall majority and is unable to form a government (other than a minority government) by itself. Britain has had coalition governments in 1915–16, 1916–22, 1931–5 and 1940–5.

Code of conduct/practice (employment and commerce)
An arrangement, usually of a voluntary nature but sometimes under statute, whereby a business or other organization adopts certain rules of behaviour, such as the police in their questioning and detention of suspects, or a trade which follows specific guidelines as to its products and its relationship with consumers.

Coeducation (education)
The system in which most schools and other educational institutions in Britain (whether state or independent) admit pupils or students of both sexes. However, some schools and colleges still operate a single-sex organization.

Cohabitation (society)
See **Common law husband/wife**.

Collective bargaining (employment)
The joint discussions between employers and trade unions, whether during a dispute or in normal negotiations, in which an attempt is made to reach agreement on wages and conditions of employment. If the system fails, matters may be referred to ACAS. The government is generally not a partner in collective bargaining.

Collective responsibility (of ministers) (government)
See **Ministerial responsibility**.

College (education)
1. An independent unit of higher education within a university structure, such as those colleges which constitute Oxford and Cambridge Universities. 2. A specialist and usually vocational institution of higher education, such as a college of art, music or agriculture. 3. A wide range of educational institutions at the further education level previously run by local authorities, but which are

now independent and self-governing bodies. 4. A college (or institute) of higher education which awards degrees. 5. The actual building or buildings in which most of these different institutions are located.

College of further education (CFE) (education)
An educational institution in a local government area, which is not in the higher education sector. Students pursue a wide range of either full-time or part-time courses at such colleges after leaving secondary school at 16. These colleges are being removed from local government control and will become independent self-governing corporations.

College (Institute) of higher education (education)
A recent development in England and Wales where existing colleges (often after amalgamation with similar colleges such as teacher-training colleges) have been upgraded to higher education status and allowed to award degrees in a range of subjects. They were previously under the control of the local council, but most have now become self-governing corporations. Those which provide research degrees may apply for university status.

Coming of age (law)
Young persons cease to be minors or infants on their 18th birthday, and legally become adults. They then possess legal rights such as making a will and owning property, voting in elections, and serving on a jury and in the armed forces. They can also marry without the consent of their parents (in Scotland at 16).

Commercial radio (media)
The common term for independent local radio stations supervised by the Radio Authority throughout Britain, which raise their operating finance from commercial companies who advertise their products on the radio.

Commercial subjects (education)
Subjects, such as shorthand, typing, accounts, computing and office management, taught at many schools and colleges of further education, which give pupils/students a knowledge of employment skills used in offices and business life generally. They are also known as business studies, and in colleges may be tied to a specific educational or professional qualification.

Commercial television (media)
The common term for the independent ITC services of ITV (Chan-

nel 3) and Channel 4, which are financed largely by the money paid by commercial companies that advertise their products on television.

Commercials, the (media)
A term commonly used to describe the advertisements for a range of commercial products on independent radio and television, which appear in the middle and at the end of programmes.

Commission for Racial Equality, the (CRE) (society and law)
The statutory organization created by the Race Relations Act 1976 which through its reports and work in applying the provisions of the Act tries to reduce racial discrimination by encouraging better race relations, promoting equality of opportunity, and setting up local race relations councils usually in urban areas of ethnic concentration.

Committal proceedings (law)
Persons charged with indictable criminal offences must first appear before the magistrates' court which, on the basis of the evidence in the case, decides whether or not to commit them to the crown court for trial. Sometimes, where crown court trial is deemed either necessary or inevitable, the magistrates hold a brief hearing on documentary evidence only. When there is doubt, or the defence wishes it, the hearing before the magistrates may amount to a full trial.

Committee stage (government)
The stage in the passage of a bill through Parliament and after its second reading when it is referred to a standing committee for detailed analysis, discussion and amendment. As an alternative it can be dealt with by the whole House of Commons sitting as a committee.

Common Agricultural Policy, the (CAP) (agriculture)
The policy of the European Community, costing some three-quarters of its total expenditure, which regulates agricultural production in the member-states and the amount, price and type of a wide range of agricultural produce. It also controls payments and subsidies for farmers.

Common Entrance, the (education)
A school-leaving examination common to all independent preparatory schools which is normally sat by boys at 13 and girls at 10 in order to gain entrance (if passed) to a public school.

Common law, the (law)
Historically, the ancient unwritten law of England, based on custom and judges' decisions in court cases, in contrast to written laws or parliamentary statutes. It was later written down, and is also known as case law since it stems from the judges' decisions in the particular cases before them. The common law tradition continues today in the law courts.

Common law husband/wife (law and society)
A husband or wife recognized only at common law and not by statute. The partners are not legally married even though they may live together as husband and wife, and share a common surname. They have no legal claims on each other in terms of inheritance and succession. The term has to some extent been replaced in recent years by that of cohabitation (living together outside marriage), and the individuals are referred to as cohabitees or cohabitants.

Commoner (society)
Strictly, all persons who are not members of the royal family, but the term may also be used to specify those who do not belong to the nobility or senior peerage.

Commonwealth (of Nations), the (politics)
A worldwide organization of some 48 former and present British colonies. They accept the British sovereign as the head of the Commonwealth, but have no central governing body or common laws. The Commonwealth has a Secretariat in London (headed by the Secretary-General of the Commonwealth), holds Commonwealth conferences and sporting games, and has many exchange programmes and trade agreements between the various member-nations.

Communist Party, the (politics)
See **Democratic Left**.

Community care (society)
A controversial social welfare policy of the Conservative government which releases long-term hospital patients into the care of local authorities, and encourages such patients and the elderly to live at home, with their families, or in special accommodation. The idea is to allow local authorities to take charge of such people in a variety of ways in the community, so that they do not become institutionalized and isolated. But the policy has attracted much criticism and has had implementation problems.

Community charge, the (finance)
Commonly known as the poll tax, this local tax replaced the former
system of property-owning rates in Scotland (1989) and in England
and Wales (1990). All residents in a property over the age of 18
had to pay a flat rate tax, irrespective of income, although there
were rebates for certain people such as those on low incomes. A
controversial system, it was abolished from 1993 and replaced by a
council tax based on property values and assuming that 2 people
lived in a property.

Community council (government)
A local government unit in Wales that has replaced a number of
former structures, and which has small-scale responsibilities within
the county council organization. Scotland also has community councils at local government level, but these have minor advisory functions.

Community home (law)
A specialist residential centre or house to which a local authority
may legally commit young people (under 17) if it considers that
they are in moral danger, are beyond the control of their parents
or guardians, have been neglected or ill-treated, or have committed
criminal offences.

Community service (law)
Convicted criminal offenders over the age of 16 (17 in Northern
Ireland) who are guilty of an imprisonable offence may, with their
consent, be given community service orders by the court instead of
a custodial sentence. This means that a number of hours over a
period of a year are spent on unpaid work of various kinds in the
local community, such as repairing and decorating property.

Commuter (transport and society)
A person who travels a considerable distance, by train or other
form of transport, to and from a place of work each day. Such
commuters tend to live in the countryside or in smaller commuter
towns outside the large cities (such as London, Birmingham, Liverpool and Manchester) where they are employed.

Comprehensive school (education)
A non-selective state secondary school in England and Wales for
children (normally from the ages of 11 to 16/18) of all intellectual
abilities and social backgrounds in a local area, and to which some
90 per cent of all secondary schoolchildren in the age groups go.

A similar system operates in Scotland, but Northern Ireland has retained a partly selective system of schooling. (Some 7.5 per cent of secondary schoolchildren in England and Wales attend independent schools, and some 2.5 per cent go to the remaining state grammar and secondary modern schools.)

Confederation of British Industry, the (CBI) (commerce and industry)
An independent body established in 1965 which promotes the interests of employers in private and state industrial companies and commercial businesses. It serves as an umbrella professional association (similar to the Trades Union Congress), and provides advice and assistance to its members, negotiates with government and the trade unions, and presents the views of its members to the general public.

Consensus (politics)
A term which implies agreement on a range of matters. It has usually been employed in Britain in a political sense to illustrate similar views on policy between the major political parties, relating to the mixed economy, the welfare state and employment, particularly since 1945.

Conservation area (geography)
A special area, often in a town or city and which sometimes may be private land, that contains buildings, monuments and other features of architectural or historic interest. Building projects, alterations and other development in it are strictly controlled by the local council in order to protect the existing amenities.

Conservative Party, the (politics)
The right-wing alternative to the Labour Party in British politics, which is sometimes known as the Tory Party. It has been called the Conservative Party since the 1830s, and has recently won governmental power in the general elections of 1979, 1983, 1987 and 1992. Historically it has championed free enterprise in economic matters, sought to preserve and improve existing national institutions, encouraged property-owning and been supported mainly by the business and professional members of the middle and upper classes.

Constable (law)
The lowest-ranking police officer in the British police forces, being

either a male police constable (PC) or a woman police constable (WPC).

Constituency (government)
One of the 651 parliamentary areas in the United Kingdom where registered voters elect one MP by the simple majority voting system to represent them in the House of Commons. An inhabitant of a constituency is known as a constituent, and the political parties are represented by a constituency party organization.

Constitution (government and law)
Britain does not have a written constitution contained in any one document. Its constitution is based on the common law, Acts of Parliament (statutes), conventions, some written authorities (such as Magna Carta 1215 and the Bill of Rights 1689) and European Community law.

Constitutional monarchy (government)
The British governmental system is often described as a constitutional monarchy. This means that the monarchy's authority is limited, and its official position is defined by the country's constitution. The monarch must reign according to its provisions so that legislative authority (the legal passing of Acts) rests with Parliament, and executive authority (policy-making and the implementation of laws) is vested in the sitting government, although both functions are carried on in the sovereign's name.

Consultant (medicine)
A doctor who, unlike a general practitioner (GP), specializes in one particular branch of medicine either at a state National Health Service (NHS) hospital or in private practice, or in a combination of both.

Consumers' Association, the (CA) (commerce)
An independent and influential body established in 1956 that is composed of subscriber-members. It campaigns for the rights and interests of consumers by evaluating the quality and price of goods and services, and publishes the results in its monthly magazine *Which?*.

Contempt of court (law)
A person who does not obey the instructions or ruling of a judge, such as a journalist refusing to disclose his or her source of information in court when requested, may be charged with contempt of court and imprisoned for a period of time or fined.

Continuing education (education)
A relatively new term to describe non-degree educational courses of a vocational or recreational nature for adult students in institutions of higher education.

Conurbation (geography)
An area with a dense and very large population surrounding a major city such as Birmingham, Liverpool, London, Manchester or Glasgow.

Convention (government and law)
1. A British constitutional term to describe long-standing principles and practices of government which, although not legally binding, are generally accepted as having the force of law. 2. An international agreement, such as the European Convention on Human Rights (ECHR), which governments (including the British) sign, ratify and regard as binding.

Conveyancing (law)
The legal procedure in Britain whereby domestic and commercial properties (such as houses, flats and offices) are bought and sold. The work is normally carried out by a solicitor in England and Wales, and by similar lawyers in Scotland and Northern Ireland.

Co-op (Co-operative Wholesale Society), the (commerce)
A department store owned and managed by the Co-operative Wholesale Society (CWS), a national trading and manufacturing organization (founded 1863 in England and Wales and 1868 in Scotland) originally to serve working-class customers. Many towns and cities in Britain have a Co-op selling food, clothes, furniture, electrical products and other household goods in different departments of the store. Customers of the CWS may become shareholders in the company, which also operates its own bank (the Co-operative Bank) and travel agency.

Core subjects (education)
See **National Curriculum**.

Corner shop (commerce)
A small store usually on a street corner in residential areas of a town or city, which often opens early and closes late in the day, and provides a range of goods and services for customers in the immediate neighbourhood. A feature in recent years has been the high Asian ownership of such shops.

Coronation, the (royalty)
The ancient religious ceremony in Westminster Abbey, such as that of Queen Elizabeth II in 1953, when a new sovereign is invested and the state crown is placed on his or her head by the Archbishop of Canterbury. The monarch sits on the Coronation Chair for much of this ceremony.

Coroner (law)
A local government officer (usually a doctor or lawyer) who administers an office dealing with the registration of deaths in a local area. He or she may also investigate by means of an inquest sudden, suspicious or violent deaths, and tries to determine (sometimes with the help of a jury) the cause of death. A procurator-fiscal does a similar job in Scotland.

Corporal punishment (education and law)
Corporal punishment, or the physical punishment of children, has since 1986 been abolished in all state schools, although it remains legal in the independent educational sector and in British society outside education.

Corporation (government)
The ancient title, which may still exist in some places, for a city or town council in local government.

Corporation tax (finance)
The tax paid by a commercial company on its trading profits in a financial year, with a current rate for large companies of 35 per cent and for small companies of 25 per cent. Corporation here refers to the legal procedure (incorporation) by which a company is established as a legal body.

Correspondence course (education)
An educational programme, often for an official or professional examination or qualification, which a student studies at home by means of a postal course either through an educational institution such as the Open University, or with a correspondence college which is usually a private commercial business. The student sends in completed work for assessment by tutors which is then returned with advice.

Costs (law)
The person who loses a court case, whether criminal or civil, is liable to pay the legal expenses incurred by the court and also those of the successful party.

Cottage (housing)
A small and usually attractive property, frequently in the country-side, which may be used as a permanent residence or a summer/weekend home. It is often supposed to represent the essence of Englishness.

Council estate (government and housing)
A large residential area of a town or city (sometimes on the out-skirts but also in the inner cities) comprising council houses and flats specially built and rented out to tenants by a local government authority, such as a district council.

Council for National Academic Awards, the (CNAA) (education)
An independent body which approves courses and awards degrees and other academic qualifications in institutions of higher education (such as polytechnics) outside the universities, ensuring that these are comparable in standard with those granted by the universities. Since 1987 some institutions running CNAA-approved courses have been allowed to review their own courses. The CNAA may be phased out in the near future as all polytechnics achieve university status.

Council house (government and housing)
1. A house built and rented out by a local government council, such as a district council, to low-income tenants in the local area. Such council house tenants may now buy their houses at below-market prices after two years. 2. In some British towns and cities, another name for a town or city hall which may include local government offices and serve as the headquarters of local government.

Council of Legal Education, the (law and education)
The organization in Gray's Inn, London, operated by the Senate and General Council of the Bar, which provides a one-year pro-fessional qualifying course for all students training to be barristers in England and Wales.

Council tax, the (government)
This tax replaced the poll tax (or community charge) for local government finance in 1993–4. It is payable by every homeowner in a local council area, and is based on the value of domestic property (divided into a number of price bands) and a personal element (based upon two people occupying a property). Rebates

from the tax are given to the needy, low-income groups, and single-occupancy properties.

Councillor (government)
An elected member of a local government council such as a district council or county council, who receives no pay (only expenses) and serves in a part-time capacity. The councillors decide and implement policy for their local area.

Countryside Commission, the (CC) (society)
An independent body established in 1968 to protect and improve rural areas in England (with similar organizations in Wales, Scotland and Northern Ireland). The commission supervises the national parks, areas of outstanding natural beauty, heritage coasts and national footpaths. It publishes a code of conduct (the Country Code) for visitors to the countryside, which stresses respect for rural property and the natural environment.

County (government)
An ancient territorial unit of local administration but now one of the 47 administrative areas into which England and Wales are divided for the purposes of larger-scale local government (39 in England and 8 in Wales). The equivalent areas in Scotland and Northern Ireland are known as regions.

County council (CC) (government)
The administrative authority of a county in England and Wales, consisting of elected county councillors presided over by a chairman (or leader), with its headquarters usually in a county hall located in the county capital. The council is responsible for strategic planning, transport planning, highways, traffic regulation, education, consumer protection, rubbish disposal, the police, the fire service, libraries and the personal social services in its area. A professional chief executive will normally be in charge of county council administration. Regional councils perform the same functions in Scotland and Northern Ireland.

County court (law)
The lowest of the civil courts in England, Wales and Northern Ireland, which hears cases involving relatively small amounts of money and is presided over by a county court judge or circuit judge (or a judge who may be responsible for several county courts and visits each in turn).

County cricket (sport and leisure)
Professional cricket matches played between teams representing different counties in England and Wales, which compete for the annual County Championship (usually sponsored by a commercial company) in the cricket season (April to September). There are 18 county teams which contest matches over the traditional three- or four-day period. One-day matches are also played by county sides in special competitions.

County school (education)
A state school (primary and secondary) in England and Wales which is controlled and financially maintained by the local education authority (LEA) of the county council; 78 per cent of all state primary and secondary schools are of this type. The remaining 22 per cent of schools are known as voluntary schools.

Court of Appeal (law)
The appeal court covering England and Wales, which is located in London. It is divided into two Divisions (Criminal and Civil) and is the stage of appeal between the lower courts and the House of Lords. In Scotland the Court of Session (civil) and the High Court of Justiciary (criminal) perform similar appeal roles at this intermediate level, and Northern Ireland has its own Court of Appeal.

Covent Garden (London and the arts)
London's ancient wholesale fruit, flower and vegetable market was transferred in 1973 from its position in central London to new premises south of the River Thames and renamed New Covent Garden Market. The former site was redeveloped as shops and restaurants, but is still known as Covent Garden, as is the Royal Opera House nearby.

Cowes (Week) (sport and leisure)
A famous sailing, yachting and racing regatta held annually in August at Cowes, Isle of Wight, which attracts international competitors and is also a social occasion.

Cranwell (military)
The central military college near Cranwell, Lincolnshire (the Royal Air Force College), which trains officer cadets of the Royal Air Force, most of whom intend to graduate as pilots.

Credit card (finance)
A finance card, such as Visa, Access and Barclaycard, which is usually issued by a bank or a group of banks. The holder can

purchase goods and services on credit, which has to be repaid
(usually on a monthly basis) to the lender with interest.

Cricket (sport and leisure)
A popular summer sport for both sexes played between two teams,
each of 11 people, traditionally dressed in white clothes. They play
their matches on grass fields at the centre of which is the pitch
(playing area). One team (the batsmen) tries to score a maximum
number of runs by hitting the ball bowled (thrown) to them by the
bowler of the other team (the fielders). The fielders try to dismiss
the batsmen by catching a ball hit by a batsman before it touches
the ground or by the bowler aiming the ball so that it hits the
wicket (three wooden stumps with two smaller pieces, called
the bails, balanced on top), which the batsman has to defend with
the bat. Cricket is both an amateur and a professional game.

Criminal courts (law)
Courts of law which apply the criminal (as opposed to the civil)
law. In England and Wales the lowest is the magistrates' court,
followed by the crown court, and the Court of Appeal (Criminal
Division) in London. Northern Ireland has the same structure in
the province, while Scotland has a similar system, but with different
court names.

Criminal Investigation Department, the (CID) (law)
A specialist crime investigation unit within the British police forces,
such as that of the Metropolitan Police Force in London, which
concentrates on serious crime, like murder and major theft cases.

Criminal law (law)
The object of the criminal law is to punish (usually by fine or
imprisonment) a person accused and found guilty of a crime. Most
British crimes are defined by statute and it is usually the state which
initiates proceedings against an individual or group.

Cross examination (law)
The verbal examination by both defence and prosecution lawyers
in criminal and civil trials of a witness giving evidence in the case.

Crossbencher (government)
An independent member in both Houses of Parliament, but chiefly
in the House of Lords, who belongs neither to the government
party nor the main opposition parties. He or she sits on the
crossbenches separate from (or at right angles to) the government
and opposition benches.

Crown, the (government and royalty)
A term which historically describes both the territory (lands and property) and the authority of the sovereign. It can now sometimes be used for the sovereign as head of state, and more generally for the government in a wide sense as the voice of the monarch (head of state).

Crown court (law)
The higher criminal court (above the magistrates' court) that handles serious (indictable) offences and holds trials in the larger towns and cities throughout England and Wales. The court is under the control of a judge who may be either a judge of the High Court of Justice or a local judge. A jury of 12 citizens decides the particular case on the facts and the judge pronounces the appropriate sentence. Crown courts in Northern Ireland and the High Court of Justiciary in Scotland perform similar roles at this level.

Crown dependency (government)
A territorial possession of the British Crown, such as the Isle of Man and the Channel Islands, which is self-governing except for defence and international relations. It has its own governing bodies, law courts and educational systems. But the British government, as a Crown agent, can and does intervene if good administration is not being carried out.

Crown Prosecution Service, the (CPS) (law)
Since October 1986, the state CPS, composed of lawyers and headed by the Director of Public Prosecutions (DPP), has been responsible for the independent review and prosecution of most criminal cases instituted by police forces in England and Wales. In Scotland, responsibility for prosecution rests with the Crown Office and Procurator-Fiscal Service, and in Northern Ireland with the police and the DPP.

Cub Scouts (sport and leisure)
See **Scout Association**.

Cup Final (Football Association), the (sport and leisure)
The last match of the annual Football Association (FA) Challenge Cup competition, which takes place at Wembley Stadium in London in May. The FA Cup is an elimination or knock-out contest consisting of cup-ties (matches) between Football League and non-League teams over the football season (which runs from August to April/May).

Curate (religion)
A junior or recently ordained clergyman in the Church of England or the Roman Catholic Church who assists (or substitutes for) the permanent priest, such as a vicar or rector, in a parish.

Curriculum (education)
The detailed programme of instruction, courses, methods and books, operated by an educational institution such as a school or college.

Curriculum vitae (CV) (employment)
The record of an individual's education, professional qualifications and work experience used when applying for jobs, and which is sent to a prospective employer.

Custody (law)
The period when an accused person is not at liberty prior to a criminal trial. This may be in a prison, a remand centre or a police station cell. The actual prison sentence, if the person is found guilty, is called a custodial sentence.

Customs and Excise, the (government and finance)
The government department which collects money in the form of indirect taxes (additional to direct income tax) from individuals and organizations through Customs (tax paid on imports and exports) and Excise (tax paid on goods and services in Britain including Value Added Tax [VAT], which is a tax levied on most goods and services paid for by the consumer).

D

Dailies, the (media)
A common term for daily national newspapers in Britain which appear during the week, but not those on Sundays (which are referred to as the Sundays).

Damages (law)
The financial award in civil cases which is awarded by a court of law to a successful defendant or plaintiff against the opposite party.

Dartmouth (military)
See **Britannia Royal Naval College**.

Darts (sport and leisure)
A popular indoor game at home and in social gatherings such as the pub or working men's clubs, which has developed into a large professional entertainment business. Players throw three weighted and feathered pointed darts at a circular numbered board (dartboard), with the intention of scoring a certain number of points, depending on the particular game played.

Day boy/girl (education)
A pupil who attends an independent school, such as a boarding school, daily for his or her education, but who continues to live at home nearby rather than boarding (or living) at the school.

Day release (education and employment)
Apprentices and other young trainees are normally allowed time off from their workplace for one day a week, with pay, in order to study at a college of further education or similar institution either to gain qualifications or to learn more about their particular trade.

Deacon (religion)
The lowest ecclesiastical rank for a male before he is ordained as a priest in the Church of England and the Roman Catholic Church. The female equivalent in the Church of England and the Free Churches is called a deaconess (or sometimes deacon), but generally she can officiate only at a limited number of religious services (particularly in the Church of England).

Dean (education and religion)
1. The senior administrator in a particular section of an educational institution, such as a faculty of arts or science. 2. The Fellow of a college at Oxford or Cambridge University who handles disciplinary and some administrative matters, and occasionally student welfare. 3. A senior clergyman in the Church of England, usually with regional or diocesan administrative and religious duties.

Debit (finance)
The term to describe a bank or other financial account which owes a sum of money (in the red). The opposite is an account which is in credit (in the black).

Debit card (finance)
A plastic card (sometimes known as a direct debit card or an electronic cheque) issued by a bank which allows holders to purchase goods and services and have the cost charged direct to their bank account. Many payments in British shops and stores are now made by this method. The card can also be used to obtain money from cash dispensers outside banks.

Debrett (society)
See **Burke's Peerage**.

Decree absolute (law)
The final order made by a court judge in divorce proceedings, which means that both parties to the dissolved marriage are legally free to marry other persons.

Decree nisi (law)
The interim decision made by a court judge in divorce proceedings that a divorce will be finalized at a future date (usually six weeks afterwards) unless anyone can show sufficient reason why the divorce should not proceed.

Defence (law)
The party, known as the defendant in both criminal and civil cases, who is accused of an offence or against whom a claim is made, and who arranges a defence to the charge in legal proceedings and at any eventual trial.

Defendant (law)
See **Accused** and **Defence**.

Degree (education)
An award to a student after the successful completion of a course

at an institution of higher education, such as a BA, BSc, MA or PhD (Doctor of Philosophy). A first degree (BA or BSc) in most parts of Britain (except for Scotland where it is often an MA after four years' study) may be an Honours degree (awarded with a class 1, 2 or 3) which specializes in one subject and which normally takes three years to complete. A pass degree is not divided into honours, while a general degree (also known as an ordinary degree and lasting usually three years) involves several subjects and is not specialized.

Deindustrialization (employment and industry)
The process in Britain in recent years when the traditional heavy manufacturing industries (such as steel, coal-mining and shipbuilding) have been reduced in number and scale, leading to unemployment in the workforce. The national economy has moved from heavy industry to lighter, more diversified manufactures and the service sector trades.

Delegated legislation (government)
The procedure whereby Parliament allows ministers and civil servants to draft the details of an Act of Parliament, such as administrative regulations. This is done to save parliamentary time, and because Parliament is too busy to oversee all the details of legislation.

Democratic Left, the (politics)
Since 1991 the name by which the former Communist Party (CP) in Britain or its surviving organization is now known. The CP was founded in 1920, but has had little parliamentary success. Its membership has declined substantially and there have been several break-away parties formed, such as the Communist Party of Britain. The latter's daily newspaper, the *Morning Star*, has also suffered declining sales and undergone shifts of editorial emphasis over the years.

Denationalization (politics and government)
The economic policy, usually pursued by a Conservative government when in power, which has transferred state (or nationalized industries) to private ownership (now often called privatization and deregulation).

Denomination (religion)
A term to describe and distinguish a church or religious group in

terms of its beliefs and practices, such as the Church of England or the Roman Catholic Church.

Department (government)
An official administrative unit of the central government, such as the Departments of Education, Health, Social Security, and the Environment, which are concerned with the implementation of government policy. They have a secretary of state at their head.

Derby, the (sport and leisure)
A well known and classic annual race for 3-year-old horses held on a racecourse at Epsom Downs in Surrey, first run in 1780.

Deregulation (commerce and government)
An economic policy used by Conservative governments from 1979 onwards by which regulations and restrictions on various industries and organizations, such as bus transport and the (London) Stock Exchange, were removed. The idea is to free the particular market and to encourage competition between different sectors.

Detached house (housing)
A single house which is not joined to another building. It stands on its own land within its own boundaries. These properties are more expensive and generally more sought-after than semi-detached or terraced houses.

Devaluation (finance and government)
An economic measure which has been used in the past by the British government to decrease the value of the country's currency relative to gold or the currencies of other countries. It is usually undertaken to correct a trade deficit on the balance of payments. The object is to make exports cheaper on the world market and imports more expensive on the home market. It has not been used as a specific economic weapon in Britain since 1967, although government policies have sometimes resulted in effective devaluations.

Devolution (government)
The potential transfer of some political and economic powers from central government in the Westminster Parliament to local, regional and national areas in Britain, so that they have greater powers to organize their own affairs. Northern Ireland achieved local rule in 1921 in many areas, but this has lapsed since 1972 with the introduction of direct rule from the British government in London. It was

also proposed for Scotland and Wales in the 1970s, a proposal which remains on the political agenda.

Diocese (religion)
An administrative area (subdivided into parishes) which is centred on a cathedral in the Church of England and the Roman Catholic Church and has a bishop as its head.

Diploma (education)
A certificate awarded by an educational institution following the successful completion of a course of study, which is not a degree-awarding programme.

Diplomatic Service, the (government)
The specialist section of the Civil Service that supplies civil servants to the Foreign and Commonwealth Office and selects personnel for service in embassies, consular posts and international organizations overseas.

Direct debit (finance)
Written permission from a customer to a specific organization (such as an electricity or insurance company) which allows it to debit (or withdraw) specific amounts of money (usually monthly or annually) from the customer's bank account, and which is often used as a method to pay regular bills.

Direct rule (government)
The direct supervision and control since 1972 of many security and administrative matters in Northern Ireland by the British government (through the Northern Ireland Office), instead of these being organized and dealt with by local people in the province. This followed an upsurge of violence in Northern Ireland and the inability of the Northern Ireland government to function or carry out reforms.

Director (commerce)
A person who is appointed in an (often) executive capacity to help run with other directors a commercial company, and who is responsible for its efficient management and performance. Some directors may be appointed to non-executive or advisory positions only.

Director-General (BBC), the (DG) (media)
Appointed by the governors of the BBC, he or she is the corporation's chief executive officer, who heads the Board of Manage-

ment, which is in charge of the daily running of BBC services. The term may also be used in connection with executive figures in other institutions.

Director of Public Prosecutions, the (DPP) (law)
The government-appointed official, who is a professionally qualified lawyer and who makes the decision whether or not to bring criminal prosecutions in special, difficult or important cases. He or she also advises central government departments, chief constables and other groups about legal matters, and heads the Crown Prosecution Service (CPS).

Disestablishment (religion)
The procedure whereby an established national Church is freed from its close connections with and legal obligations to the state or Parliament. This has happened with the Anglican Church of Wales, but not the Church of England.

Dissolution (of Parliament), the (government)
The dissolution (or ending) of a Parliament legally occurs at the end of the five-year period of office of the sitting government. But dissolution frequently takes place earlier by the choice of the Prime Minister. Parliament is dissolved and writs for the resultant general election are ordered by the monarch on the advice of the Prime Minister.

District council (DC) (government)
An elected local government authority which is a subdivision of the county council structure in England and Wales. It organizes services within its area, such as sanitation, housing, planning permission and rubbish collection. It also implements the larger-scale policy decisions of the county council. There are similar district council structures in Scotland and Northern Ireland.

District Health Authority (DHA) (medicine)
Some 200 district health authorities in England and Wales are responsible for the planning and operational control of all state health services in their local areas. Health boards in Scotland, and health and social services boards in Northern Ireland, do the same job.

District nurse (medicine)
A qualified nurse, usually employed by a district health authority, who provides medical treatment for people in their homes, and who has responsibility for a specific local area.

Dividend (finance)
A variable sum of money which is paid regularly (normally twice in a financial year) from the trading profits of a commercial company to its shareholders. If trade or the profits are bad, no dividend may be payable.

Division (government and sport and leisure)
1. The occasion for a formal vote in the House of Commons, when MPs cast their votes either for a motion or against it in one of two Yes and No corridors or division lobbies. 2. Professional football clubs play in one of the three divisions of the English Football League. A new Premier League with 22 clubs replaced the existing First Division in 1992. There are similar divisions in Scotland and Northern Ireland. 3. Counties in England and Wales (and regions in Scotland and Northern Ireland) are divided into electoral divisions for local government purposes, with each returning one councillor or more in county and regional elections.

Division of powers (government)
A term which is sometimes used to describe the different functions of the executive, legislature and judiciary in the British constitutional system.

Divisional court, the (law)
A special branch of the Queen's Bench Division of the High Court in England and Wales which usually hears appeals on matters of law from the magistrates' court and the crown court in criminal law, and sometimes from the county court in civil law. It can also decide legal matters of a constitutional and administrative nature.

Divorce (law)
The dissolution of a marriage by court order, on application by either party. Since 1969, the only ground necessary for divorce is that the marriage has irretrievably broken down, as shown by examples of adultery, separation, desertion or unreasonable behaviour. The court will determine issues like the custody of any children, distribution of property, and the payment of maintenance by one party to another. The divorce decree comes in two stages (decree nisi and decree absolute) after which the parties are free to marry other people.

D-notice (media and government)
A directive (D standing for defence), established in 1912, to media organizations by the government advising against the publication of

particular security and defence information. Any acceptance of this advice amounts to a form of voluntary self-censorship by the media, since they are not legally obliged to obey the directive.

Doctor (medicine)
See **General practitioner** and **Consultant**.

Doctor of Philosophy (PhD) (education)
A doctoral degree granted by an institution of higher education to a student who has completed a research thesis in either arts or science subject-areas.

Documentary (media)
A programme, usually on television, which examines the facts of a particular issue in depth, and attempts to reach objective conclusions.

Do-it-yourself (DIY) (sport and leisure)
A popular and relatively cheap British pastime of personally making improvements and repairs to a house without the help of professional painters, carpenters and builders. Specialized DIY shops sell the necessary equipment and materials.

Donor card (medicine)
An identification card which is carried on an individual's person and which gives legal authority to a hospital to use parts of his or her body for transplant and other surgery on death, whether by accident or natural causes.

Double (sport and leisure)
1. When the dart (in a darts match) lands in the double ring round the outer edges of a dartboard, it scores twice the number of points. 2. A bet which is placed on two horses in different horse-races, with any winnings from the first race being placed automatically on the second. 3. A football team which wins both the English FA Cup and the Football League title in one season. May also be used in other sports.

Double-decker (transport)
A bus with room for passengers on two decks (or levels), used widely throughout Britain by local transport authorities. Standing-room is confined to the lower deck.

Downing Street (government)
A street in central London, off Whitehall, which contains the official

government homes of the Prime Minister (No. 10) and the Chancellor of the Exchequer (No. 11).

Driver and Vehicle Licensing Agency, the (DVLA) (transport)
The government agency in Swansea, Wales, operated by the Department of Transport and staffed by civil servants, which issues vehicle and driving licences for vehicles to people throughout Britain, and keeps their records. A full driving licence is issued to a car driver at 17 after passing a driving test and is valid until the age of 70. A provisional licence is normally issued for use only while a driver is learning to drive under instruction or when accompanied by a fully qualified driver.

Drought (geography)
A period of dry conditions resulting from a lack of rainfall or depletion of water reserves, which has occurred frequently in Britain in recent years. It can cause problems for farmers, the water companies and the general public, and an official drought is defined as a period of at least 15 days on none of which more than 0.25 mm of rain has fallen.

Drury Lane (arts and London)
London's oldest functional theatre founded in 1663, formally called the Theatre Royal, and well known for its musicals and other light entertainment.

Dubbing (media)
The technical process whereby the original foreign language in a film or television programme is changed to an English-speaking sound-track.

Duchy of Cornwall, the (royalty)
The duchy (land and property belonging to a duke or duchess) created in Cornwall in 1337. Traditionally the duchy has been granted to the eldest son of the sovereign (at present Prince Charles) who holds the title Duke of Cornwall and receives income from and manages the property and business interests of the duchy.

Duchy of Lancaster, the (government)
A duchy (land and property belonging to a duke or duchess) created in Lancashire in 1399 and nominally held by the Chancellor of the Duchy of Lancaster. The Chancellor is a minister in the Cabinet, but has few departmental duties and may be given special additional responsibilities by the Prime Minister.

Duke of Edinburgh, the (royalty)
The title of Prince Philip, the husband of Queen Elizabeth II, which was granted after his marriage in 1947. He has no official constitutional role in the British system, but is well known for his interest in the problems of British industry and his encouragement of young people through the Duke of Edinburgh's Award Scheme (founded in 1956).

E

Easter (religion)
A central religious occasion for Christians in Britain, celebrating the resurrection of Christ and focusing on Easter Sunday (or Easter Day), which occurs between 22 March and 25 April. Easter eggs, today made of chocolate, have been traditionally eaten to symbolize new life and springtime. The following day is called Easter Monday and is a bank holiday.

Economic and Monetary Union (EMU) (finance)
The process whereby the members of the European Community (EC) are attempting to integrate their economic and monetary systems by the adoption, following the creation of a single European market, of a common currency and European Bank.

Edinburgh (geography)
The capital of Scotland with a population of 420,000, well known for its elegant and historic buildings (such as Edinburgh Castle where the Edinburgh Military Tattoo is held annually) and for the yearly Edinburgh Festival. It is a university city, administrative centre and cultural venue.

Edinburgh Festival, the (arts)
An annual cultural festival of music, drama, dance and the arts, established in 1947 and held in August and September in Edinburgh. It has an international reputation and is particularly well known for the Edinburgh Fringe or experimental dramatic and other artistic presentations.

Editorials (media)
Specially written pieces, whether by the editor or editorial staff, in a newspaper which comment upon specific items of topical interest and often state the paper's point of view on a range of issues. These mostly appear as leading articles on an editorial page.

Education Committee (education)
The special committee of councillors, usually of an English or Welsh county council, which co-ordinates educational policy for the state

schools in the local government area with the local education
authority (LEA).

Eisteddfod (arts)
An annual Welsh celebration of music, literature and drama (the
Royal National Eisteddfod) performed in Welsh in August. A well
known aspect of the festival is the investiture of the winning bard
or poet in a poetry competition. The term is also employed for other
music, language and folk-dancing festivals in Wales and England.

Either-way offences (law)
Criminal offences, such as theft, which are both summary and
indictable. This means that the matter can be tried in the magistrates' court with the accused's consent. But if the magistrates
consider that the offence is too serious for their competence, they
will order that it be heard in the crown court and the accused has
no choice in the matter.

Elective dictatorship (government)
A term coined by Lord Hailsham (a former Lord Chancellor) to
describe the potential results of the British parliamentary electoral
system. This can give a government an overall majority of seats in
the House of Commons with a minority of the popular vote, which
enables it to carry its legislative programme and policies through
Parliament with no effective opposition.

Electoral register (politics and government)
The official record (also known as the register of voters) which
contains information about people registered in a parliamentary
constituency and who are able to vote in a parliamentary general or
by-election. The register is drawn up annually by local government
officials to include new voters and to exclude people who have died
or moved away from the constituency, and is kept in the local
authority offices.

Electorate, the (politics)
The body of voters in Britain (some 43.7 million people) who are
eligible to vote in general and by-elections, and a slightly higher
number in local elections.

Electricity supplies, the (science and commerce)
British electricity supplies were privatized (except for nuclear
power) in 1990–1 (with Northern Ireland in 1991–2). The National
Grid Company now operates the bulk transfer of electricity across
the national grid (or network) in England and Wales, and together

with 12 regional companies and the two main generators (National Power and Power-Gen) is responsible for the production, sale and distribution of electricity. Similar structures also apply in Scotland and Northern Ireland. The Office of Electricity Regulations (Offer) is the independent regulator of the electricity supplies following privatization.

Eleven-plus, the (education)
The national school examination that was previously used in England and Wales to select which pupils at the age of 11 should receive a secondary education at an academic grammar school, a non-academic secondary modern school, or a technical school. This selective regime has been replaced by the comprehensive system, although selection procedures (if not the 11-plus) are still operated by a small minority of local education authorities (LEAs) which retain grammar schools.

Employment Training (ET) (employment)
A government scheme established by the Conservatives in 1988, which replaced earlier programmes, and provides individually adapted training and retraining programmes for the longer-term unemployed. Training is carried out under contract by local training and enterprise councils (TECs) in England and Wales and local enterprise companies (LECs) in Scotland.

England (geography)
The biggest country in Britain in terms of both land and population (46.1 million), with Wales lying at its western, and Scotland at its northern, borders. The capital of the United Kingdom (London) is in the south-east. It is the centre of the British governmental system, and contains the head offices of national institutions and businesses.

English Heritage (government)
The Historic Buildings and Monuments Commission for England (English Heritage) is a recently established government body (1984) which preserves and protects listed monuments and buildings in England that are of historic, architectural or archaeological interest, such as Stonehenge (an ancient collection of standing stones in Wiltshire whose origin and purpose are debated) and Hadrian's Wall (an old Roman protective barrier between Scotland and England). Similar organizations exist in the rest of Britain.

English Stage Company, the (ESC) (arts)
An influential theatre company which was established in 1956 and

has its headquarters at the well known Royal Court (Theatre) in
London. It is noted for its innovative and experimental plays by
new and young dramatists, as well as its contemporary foreign
drama productions.

Enterprise zones (employment, commerce and government)
Programmes established by the Conservative government at various
intervals since 1981 and running for 10 years, which pinpoint urban
areas of economic decay and attempt to revitalize them by giving
financial grants and tax exemptions to firms willing to relocate in
the zones. There are now 27 of them, located in London, the
Midlands, South Wales, northern England, central Scotland and
Northern Ireland.

Epsom (Downs) (sport and leisure)
A well known racecourse near Epsom, Surrey, where the classic
horse-races (the Derby and the Oaks) and other races are run each
year in the horse-racing season.

Equal Opportunities Commission, the (EOC) (government)
A government organization established in 1975 which attempts to
reduce sex discrimination and to create better and more equal
opportunities for men and women in a range of activities such as
employment, services and education. The commission monitors the
workings of the Equal Pay Act 1970 and the Sex Discrimination
Act 1975, which are intended respectively to prevent discrimination
between men and women and to enforce equal rates of pay for
similar work done by both sexes.

Equal Pay Act 1970, the (employment)
See **Equal Opportunities Commission**.

Establishment, the (society)
A somewhat vague and debatable term to describe the leading
sectors of British society, such as industrialists and business leaders,
politicians, the aristocracy, the professions and the Church of
England, which are collectively supposed to organize British society
and to influence the people by the dissemination of dominant
values.

Estate agency (commerce and housing)
A private professional firm that advertises houses, flats, land and
other property for sale or purchase, both in the domestic and
commercial markets. Estate agents in England and Wales cannot
at present complete the actual legal transactions of sale and

purchase which is the job of a solicitor, whereas in Scotland a lawyer will do all the necessary work including that of an estate agent.

Ethnic communities, the (society)
A term to describe those minority communities in Britain, such as Asians, West Indians and Pakistanis (among others), who have different ethnic or racial origins from the majority of the indigenous population.

Euro-MP (government)
One of 81 British MEPs (Members of the European Parliament) chosen by direct elections in Britain (as in 1979, 1984 and 1989) to represent a British political party and constituency (which is larger than and different from the usual British parliamentary constituency) in the European Parliament, the representative body of the European Community (EC).

European Community (EC), the (government)
The European organization of 12 member-states which Britain joined formally in 1973. A referendum (the first in British history) on continued membership was held by the Labour government in 1975, and a majority (2 to 1) were in favour of Britain remaining in the EC. Britain's membership has been difficult, but it is now tied to Europe in practical and legal ways. Britain has representatives on the European Commission, the Council of Ministers, the European Court of Justice, and in the European Parliament.

European Community Law (law)
An addition to traditional British law as a result of membership of the European Community. Such law (in the form of regulations and directives) now takes precedence over British domestic law in specific areas, and where there is a conflict between the two systems.

European Convention on Human Rights, the (ECHR) (law)
The international agreement which Britain has signed and ratified. British citizens who feel aggrieved because of an alleged breach of their human rights and who cannot obtain satisfaction in the British courts can take their case to the European Commission of Human Rights which may forward the case to the European Court of Human Rights in Strasbourg (not part of the EC), although the process is lengthy and expensive. The British government is morally

obliged to recognize and implement any decision which goes against it.

European Court of Justice, the (ECJ) (law and government)
The Court of Justice of the European Community has a central and important role in the working of the EC. It consists of judges of the member-states; it safeguards and rules on the provisions of the Treaty of Rome; and it settles disputes concerning European Community law. Individuals, member-states and the EC may bring cases before the ECJ, which may rule against national governments and Parliaments.

Eventing (sport and leisure)
An equestrian (horse-riding) competition over several days (usually three) that normally consists of dressage (which tests the obedience of horses), cross-country riding and show-jumping (in the ring). The most important meeting in Britain is the Badminton Horse Trials, where eventing originated in 1949.

Examination boards (school) (education)
Independent bodies (such as the Northern Examination and Assessment Association which accounts for some one-third of all pupils taking examinations) that set and arrange the marking of the national examinations in England and Wales for the GCSE, A-level and AS-level examinations. Examination boards exist in Scotland and Northern Ireland for similar purposes, and there are others at Oxford and Cambridge which cater for a wide range of national and overseas examinations.

Exchange Rate Mechanism (European), the (ERM) (finance)
The system of monetary control within the European Monetary System (EMS), which Britain joined in 1990. The ERM is intended to stabilize the currencies of member-states by setting (aligning) them at certain levels and usually pegging them to a strong currency such as the German mark. The system was under considerable pressure in 1992, and Britain was forced into a (temporary) suspension of membership.

Ex-directory (communications)
A personal telephone number, known only to selected people, which does not appear in the public and official telephone directory published by British Telecom (BT), because of an individual's desire to preserve privacy.

Executive, the (government)
A constitutional term referring to the sitting British government
(composed of the Cabinet, ministers, departments and ministries)
which initiates and implements national policies for the whole of
the United Kingdom.

F

Fabian Society, the (politics)
A political association established in 1884 which is still active and has a current membership of some 3,500. Its socialist manifesto, publications and political campaigns contributed to the political and intellectual conditions in which the Labour Party was formally founded in 1906.

Family credit (finance)
A state benefit in the social security system which is paid to families in employment with low wages (including one-parent families) and having at least one child. The total sum for a family is dependent upon its level of income and savings and the number and ages of the children.

Family Division (of the High Court), the (law)
The division of the High Court which deals mainly with domestic or matrimonial cases, such as divorce, the financial and property arrangements after divorce, the welfare of the children of the family, adoption and guardianship.

Fastnet Race, the (sport and leisure)
A well known yachting contest which attracts international competitors and takes place every two years in August on an ocean course of some 670 miles (1,085 km) from the Isle of Wight, around the Fastnet Rock off south-west Ireland, and returning to Plymouth, Devon.

Father of the House, the (government)
The honorary title given to the longest continuously serving MP in the House of Commons or peer in the House of Lords. He or she has only a limited number of formal functions.

Fee-paying (education)
The term describing the money (fees) that is paid, usually by the parents, to educate a child at an independent school. This may amount to several thousand pounds a year and varies considerably between schools.

Fellow (education)
A teaching or non-teaching member of a college at Oxford and Cambridge Universities, and an academic elsewhere who has been awarded a fellowship to pursue research. The term is also used to describe certain elected members of a learned society, such as the Royal Society (RS) and the British Academy (BA).

Field sports (sport and leisure)
The traditional rural sports of hunting, shooting and fishing which take place in the open countryside and are associated with the gentry and country life.

Fifth form (education)
The class in a secondary school (whether state or independent) in which 16-year-old pupils normally take the GCSE examination in England and Wales, and in which many finish their compulsory school education. They are in their fifth year at the school, which most will have entered at 11 years of age.

Fifth of November, the (society)
See **Guy Fawkes' Night**.

Finals (education)
The name for the final examinations of a first degree at an institution of higher education usually taken in the third year of a three-year course.

Finance house (finance)
A private commercial company which lends money to clients at variable rates of interest to finance their hire-purchase agreements and other loan arrangements.

Financial Times Index, the (FT Index) (finance)
Details of the daily movement (or change in the price) of most shares on the (London) Stock Exchange published by the *Financial Times*, an influential daily national quality newspaper founded in 1888, which specializes in financial information.

Financial Times-Stock Exchange 100 Index, the (FT-SE) (finance)
The stocks and shares index introduced in 1984 by the (London) Stock Exchange, commonly known as the Footsie. It records the daily movement (or price change) of the shares of 100 prominent companies.

Financial year, the (finance)
The period (also known as the income tax year) beginning on

6 April and ending on 5 April in the following year, for which the government sets its annual tax policies and estimates. It represents the income tax year for individuals, during which they are charged income tax on their earnings and investments. Companies, partnerships and other business concerns may have a different financial year depending on choice.

Fines (law)
The amount of money that a person convicted of a criminal offence is required to pay to the court instead of (or in addition to) imprisonment. The large majority of punishments in British courts are fines.

First class (transport, communications and education)
1. The most expensive class of seat in a passenger train operated by British Rail. 2. The more expensive of two postal rates operated by the Post Office (the other being second class) which is supposed to guarantee next-day delivery of mail (with the exception of Sundays). 3. The top class of an honours degree (a first) at an institution of higher education.

First floor, the (society)
In Britain, this is the next floor above the ground floor, usually in a multi-storey building.

First-past-the-post system (politics)
The commonly used term to illustrate the operation of the British election system. The constituency candidate at a parliamentary election who achieves the largest number of votes (a simple majority), wins the election and the seat, even if the majority is only one. Similarly the party which achieves the greatest number of parliamentary seats in the House of Commons wins the election and its leader will usually be invited by the monarch to form the government.

First reading (government)
The formal and brief introduction of a draft bill into Parliament (usually in the House of Commons). This initial step is followed by the second and third readings, and the report and committee stages, in the bill's legislative passage through the Houses of Parliament.

Flat (housing)
A self-contained living unit in both the public and the private housing sectors which can vary in size, with one or more bedrooms

and other utility rooms, normally on the same floor. Flats are usually located in a converted house or specially constructed blocks.

Flat, the (sport and leisure)
The name of that part of the horse-racing season which is concerned with racing on a flat racecourse, in contrast to steeplechasing which is run over obstacles (jumps or fences).

Fleet Street (London and media)
The well known street in central London which until the late 1980s was the centre of the national newspaper industry and where most newspapers had their headquarters. They have now left the street for other sites in the capital, such as Wapping in East London, but the term 'Fleet Street' is still synonymous with national papers.

Flotation (finance)
The procedure whereby shares in a new public company are offered for sale (or floated) on the (London) Stock Exchange.

Flying Squad, the (law)
A well known former section of the CID at New Scotland Yard in the London Metropolitan Police Force, which has now been disbanded. It has been replaced by an 'organized crime' branch which consists of specialist detectives who investigate large-scale criminal activities.

Football (sport and leisure)
See **Association Football**.

Football Association, the (FA) (sport and leisure)
The independent organization established in 1863 and with its headquarters in London which officially controls all professional and amateur association football (clubs and teams) in Britain, through national and regional associations in Scotland, England, Wales and Northern Ireland. The new (1992) Premier League for top professional clubs in England is organized by the FA.

Football League, the (FL) (sport and leisure)
The independent body established in 1888 that controls the playing structure of most of the major professional football matches in Britain. The English league is made up of football clubs and divided into three divisions (two in the Scottish League) and is based on promotion and relegation for teams at the end of each football season. A Premier League consisting of 22 clubs was introduced in England in 1992 which replaced the existing First Division, and

which is organized by the Football Association not the Football League. There is a similar Premier League in Scotland.

Foreign and Commonwealth Office, the (FCO) (government)
The government department, headed by the Foreign Secretary and staffed by civil servants, that is in charge of Britain's foreign relations with other countries including Commonwealth nations, negotiates with the European Community and advises the government on foreign policy.

Foreign Exchange Market, the (finance)
The market is based largely in the City (of London), although it has no one fixed location. Instead specialist foreign exchange dealers buy and sell currencies on the foreign currency exchanges by telephone from stockbrokers', banks' or other corporate offices in the City.

Foreign Secretary, the (government)
The Secretary of State for Foreign and Commonwealth Affairs, who is head of the Foreign and Commonwealth Office, a Cabinet member, and central figure in the government. He or she is responsible for the initiation and implementation of Britain's foreign policy.

Forestry Commission, the (FC) (government)
The official government organization (established in 1919) which supervises the 50 per cent of British forests which are state-owned. The other half are privately owned, and the commission is empowered to advise and give financial aid to private owners to encourage the better management and utilization of such forests. It also controls specially designated forest parks (11 in Great Britain and 9 in Northern Ireland), to which the public have access.

Forms (education)
Classes in British secondary schools are normally called forms, starting with the first form at the age of 11 and extending to the sixth form (usually divided into upper and lower) for 16–18-year-olds.

Foundation subjects (education)
See **National Curriculum**.

Fourth estate, the (media)
A historical name for the press (newspapers), in the sense that it has been seen as an unofficial influence in national affairs and a former of public opinion. The House of Lords has been traditionally

regarded as the first estate, the House of Commons as the second and the Church of England as the third.

Franchise (commerce)
A commercial arrangement in which an independent business is granted a licence to run part (or sell products) of a larger concern, such as the independent television companies which bid for ITC franchises and are awarded a licence to provide programmes for a given area under the supervision of the ITC.

Free Churches, the (religion)
Most of those Protestant Churches or sects in Britain which are not Anglican or Roman Catholic by denomination, and which have their own doctrines and forms of worship. They were originally called Dissenters and Nonconformists because they did not conform to the teaching and practices of either of the major Christian Churches, and today are free in the sense that they are not established like the Church of England. They include (among others) the Methodist Church, the Baptists and the United Reformed Church.

Free paper (media)
A weekly local newspaper, delivered to homes throughout Britain without cost to the recipient. It largely consists of advertisements (which pay the costs of publishing) but also carries some local news and feature articles.

Freedom of the city, the (society)
An honorary title given to a distinguished individual who is closely identified, either by birth or achievements, with a particular city, and who is then called a Freeman of that city.

Freefone (communications)
One of the specialist telephone facilities provided by British Telecom (BT) that allows an individual to make a telephone call without charge to commercial and other organizations, which pay for the costs themselves.

Freepost (communications)
One of the specialist mail facilities provided by the Post Office (PO) that allows an individual to send letters without charge to a business organization, which pays for the cost itself.

Fresher (education)
The short name (for freshman/woman) given to first-year students in institutions of higher education. It has traditionally been mostly associated with universities.

Friendly Society (finance)
An insurance association (also known as a Provident Society), to which members pay subscriptions over a period of time and from which they receive financial help when needed, such as in sickness, widowhood and old age. These societies historically provided assistance to low-income employees, but today supply many other forms of insurance, pensions and investment schemes.

Fringe (Edinburgh), the (arts)
See **Edinburgh Festival**.

Front benches, the (government)
The two rows of front seats in the House of Commons, immediately to the right and left of the Speaker's Chair. Those on the Speaker's right contain the ministers (and Prime Minister) of the sitting government, while those on the left are occupied by the leading members (Shadow Cabinet) of the Official Opposition. Such MPs are known as frontbenchers in contrast to the backbenchers who sit behind them.

Fund-holder (medicine)
See **General practitioner**.

Further education (FE) (education)
A term that describes any formal education which an individual follows after leaving secondary school at the age of 16, but which is not degree-level work at the higher education institutions. Such educational courses are normally provided by local colleges of further education (CFEs) which were previously under the control of the local government educational authority, but which are now self-governing and independent.

G

Gala (sport and leisure)
A holiday occasion which may involve a range of leisure activities, sports events or parades, such as the annual Durham Miners' Gala in July in the north of England which has brass bands and political speeches by Labour Party and trade union representatives.

Gangway, the (government)
The passageway between the benches in the House of Commons midway down the chamber, and away from the Speaker's Chair. An MP who chooses to sit here, and consequently at some distance from the Speaker and the front benches, is supposed to hold independent political views and may be in conflict with his or her party.

Garden city (society)
A term associated with the initial development of New Towns in Britain in the early twentieth century. They were specially designed with parks, gardens and open spaces, and were usually built in the countryside or Green Belt areas. The first garden city was established in 1903 at Letchworth, Hertfordshire.

Gatwick Airport (transport)
The second-largest international airport in Britain (after Heathrow), in West Sussex, south of London. It handles scheduled and charter passenger flights as well as freight services.

General Assembly of the Church of Scotland, the (religion)
The highest governing council of the Church of Scotland for administrative, religious and policy matters, comprising ministers, elders and elected members of the Church. Its leader, elected for one year, is the Moderator of the Church of Scotland, who acts as the spokesperson for the Church.

General Certificate of Secondary Education, the (GCSE) (education)
The main school-leaving examination, introduced in 1988 and taken by secondary schoolchildren at the age of 15 or 16 in England and Wales. It is closely connected to the new National Curriculum. GCSE certificates are awarded for each subject passed on a scale from A to G and the examination is administered by six groups of

independent examining boards, such as the Northern Examination and Assessment Association. The final grade is composed of marks for project work spread over the two-year course and of written examinations.

General election (politics and government)
A parliamentary election held, following a dissolution of Parliament, in the United Kingdom on an election day (usually a Thursday) to elect constituency MPs to parliamentary seats in the House of Commons. The electors vote at polling stations in the appropriate local wards of the constituency in which they are registered. A government is usually formed from the party which obtains a majority of the parliamentary seats.

General hospital (medicine)
A state National Health Service (NHS) hospital, which is frequently a large urban building with emergency facilities, and which caters for a wide range of patients (including out-patients) and diseases. Most hospitals are organized by local district, regional or board health authorities, but some have now opted-out of this system and become self-governing trusts receiving their finance direct from central government.

General practitioner (GP) (medicine)
A qualified doctor who is not a specialist or consultant, but who has a general medical practice (often in a group practice at a health centre) in which most types of illnesses may be treated. However, some GPs still practise on their own. Although employed by the state (or local health authority) GPs may have a number of private patients who pay for their own treatment. Some GPs, usually in group practices, have become 'fund-holding' doctors under Conservative government reforms. This means that they are given a budget from central government, and may themselves choose how to spend it, including buying services and treatment for their patients at local hospitals.

Gentry, the (society)
A term, which is now largely of historical interest but is still occasionally used, for those minor members of the aristocracy with a social position below the nobility (royalty and peers).

Geological Museum, the (GM) (science)
The national scientific museum concerned with the earth's history,

founded in 1837 and based in London. It contains an extensive collection of minerals, fossils and other geological objects.

Gilbert and Sullivan Operas, the (arts)
Comic, and frequently satiric, operettas written in the nineteenth century by the composer Sir Arthur Sullivan and the librettist Sir William Gilbert. They were originally performed (1875–96) at the Savoy (Theatre), London, and have since been staged by professional theatres and amateur groups. They have become a popular British (English) institution.

Gilt-edged securities (finance)
Government stocks and shares (commonly known as gilts) traded on the (London) Stock Exchange, whose capital and interest are guaranteed by the government. Although their price may fluctuate, they are regarded as a secure investment and likely to generate a good interest.

Ginger group (society)
A small group of members within an organization that attempts to provoke or pressurize the larger body into more decisive action.

Giro system, the (finance)
A system, established in 1968 when the Post Office formed its own National Girobank (since privatized), whereby money is transferred between banks by means of a bank giro credit arrangement. Giro cheques, such as those paying unemployment benefit or income support, can be sent through the system and may also be cashed at a post office.

Glyndebourne (arts)
A well known, privately financed annual opera festival, established in 1934, which takes place at a country house in East Sussex, and is a popular summer musical and social occasion.

Golden handshake (employment)
The commonly used term to describe the (normally) considerable amount of money which is paid to a senior employee in a commercial company on retirement in recognition of past services, or sometimes on the dismissal of a director or senior manager as compensation for the loss of the job.

Good Friday (religion)
The Friday before Easter Sunday (Easter Day), and a bank holiday in Britain, when the Christian churches commemorate the Crucifixion of Christ.

Goodwill (commerce)
An asset of a business which cannot easily be quantified, such as a good reputation and established customer and trading relations, but which is now less frequently used. It can, however, be important when determining the value of a business, especially when incorporating an assessment of goodwill into the sale price.

Go-slow (employment)
An industrial dispute or action by the workforce of a factory or other business which deliberately slows down the employees' work rate and hence the rate of production in that business.

Gossip column (media)
A feature (often in the form of a diary) written by a columnist (or reporter) in a newspaper (usually a popular paper) or magazine which provides the latest information, rumours and scandal about prominent public figures and celebrities.

Government (government)
The executive branch (including the Cabinet) of the British constitutional system, which initiates and determines political policy. It comprises ministers and secretaries of state who head the various ministries and departments responsible for implementing government decisions.

Government Communications Headquarters, the (GCHQ) (military)
The government intelligence centre at Cheltenham, Gloucestershire, which gathers, collates and analyses military and other information from many different sources around the world.

Governor (society, education and law)
1. The formal title of the chief official with executive responsibility for an institution such as a prison governor or the Governor of the Bank of England. 2. An appointed or elected member of an educational governing body, such as that of a university, college or school, responsible for the administration, policies and priorities of the institution.

Graduate (education)
An individual who has been awarded a degree (usually a first degree) from an institution of higher education, after having passed the final examination on a course of study.

Grammar school (education)
Some grammar schools have an ancient history in England as part

of the independent sector. State grammar schools at the secondary level were created by the 1944 Education Act and provided an academic training for those pupils between the ages of 11 and 18 who had passed the 11-plus examination, and who wished to enter higher education or the professions. Today the state grammar schools have been largely replaced by the comprehensive school system and only a small minority of state school pupils attend the remaining grammar schools.

Grand National, the (sport and leisure)
A well known and prominent annual steeplechase in British horse-racing, established in 1839. It is run on the Aintree racecourse near Liverpool, and is very popular with the public who place bets on the result. It has a series of hazardous jumps or fences such as Becher's Brook and Valentine's Brook, which can cause injuries to both horses and riders if they fall at the obstacles.

Grant (education and government)
A general term for any sum of money given (or granted) to an individual or organization. It is used particularly for the finance given to local government by central government, and by local education authorities to students in higher education through the student grant.

Grassroots (society)
A term which refers to the majority of the British population who are not in positions of prominence or influence in society, but whose opinions are usually taken into account by political and other leaders. A protest movement is sometimes said to stem from the grassroots.

Great Britain (GB) (geography and government)
A political or constitutional term to describe the biggest island of the British Isles, comprising England, Scotland and Wales. Strictly speaking, the term does not include Northern Ireland which is, however, part of the United Kingdom of Great Britain and Northern Ireland.

Great Ormond Street (medicine)
The short name of the Great Ormond Street Hospital for Sick Children in central London, from the street of the same name. The hospital has a worldwide reputation for its specialism in and treatment of sick children.

Great Seal, the (government)
The official insignia (symbol or sign) of the United Kingdom which is embossed (or placed) on important (usually constitutional and legal) documents and is under the jurisdiction of the Lord Chancellor.

Greater London (London)
The local government administrative area established in 1963 which comprised the old nineteenth-century county of London and most of the former county of Middlesex together with parts of adjacent counties, under the central control of the Greater London Council (GLC). Although the GLC was abolished in 1986 the term Greater London is still used to describe London as a whole. It is now divided into the City (of London) and 32 London boroughs, covers an area of 610 square miles (1,580 sq. km), and has a current population of some 6.4 million.

Green belt (geography)
An area of agricultural land, parks, open countryside or woodland around a town or city (such as a New Town), in which no building work or urban development is permitted.

Green Cross Code, the (transport)
See **Highway Code**.

Green paper (government)
A green-coloured consultative document published by the government which contains proposals for future government policy on a specific topic. It will be discussed and responded to by interested parties both inside and outside Parliament.

Green Party, the (politics)
A political party established in 1973, becoming known as the Ecology Party, but changing its name in 1985 to the Green Party and commonly known as the Greens, with a current membership of some 6,000. Its programme is now mainly devoted to nuclear-free environmental issues, but it is not represented in the House of Commons. It is seen more as a pressure group than a political party, and many of its environmental policies have been taken up by the mainline parties.

Greenwich Mean Time (GMT) (geography)
The time-zone marked by the 0° meridian (of longitude) which passes through Greenwich, south-east of central London. It serves

as the basis for British standard time and also for all the other world time-zones that are measured from Greenwich.

Greyhound-racing (sport and leisure)
A popular sport, commonly known as the dogs, held at local greyhound tracks throughout Britain. Gamblers place bets on greyhounds (thin, fast hunting dogs) which chase round the track after a mechanical hare. The Greyhound Derby is an important annual event in this sport, held at the White City stadium in London, and first run in 1927.

Gross national product, the (GNP) (finance)
The term which describes the total value of goods and services produced in Britain on an annual basis, of which the private sector accounts for nearly three-quarters. It is an important indicator of national economic performance, and the four main elements are consumer purchases, private investment, government spending and trade.

Ground floor, the (society)
In Britain, this is the bottom floor of a building at ground level. The first floor is the next one above the ground floor.

Ground rent (housing)
The sum of money which is paid for the lease (letting) of a building, such as an office block or a house. The lease may be for a number of years and the rent is normally paid half-yearly or annually.

Groundsman (sport and leisure)
A person responsible for the maintenance and preparation of a sports arena, such as a football stadium or cricket ground.

Group practice (medicine)
A medical organization (also known as a health centre or clinic) in which a number of general practitioners (GPs) share common medical and administrative facilities, although continuing to see patients in their own individual offices or surgeries. It also serves as a local health welfare centre.

Grouse shooting (sport and leisure)
The shooting of grouse (a game bird) is a traditional rural activity among the country aristocracy and landowners, normally associated with the Scottish moors on which the grouse breed and live. The permitted shooting season is between 12 August and 10 December.

Growth rate (finance)
The annual percentage figure used to describe the growth (or lack
of it) of the national economy, and which is usually determined by
the income accruing in the four quarters of the year.

Guides Association, the (sport and leisure)
A girls' organization established in 1910, with a current membership
in Britain of some 750,000. It is the female counterpart to the male
Scout Association (although girls can now join the Scouts) and its
members are divided into three sections according to age. The
youngest are the Brownie Guides (from 7 to 10), followed by the
Guides and the Ranger Guides.

Guildhall (tradition)
The ancient name, which is still used, for a town hall in some
British towns and cities, which may be associated with legal (a
magistrates' court) or local government activities. Historically it was
the trade or business hall of a medieval guild (an association of
skilled craftsmen), a town corporation (council) or a group of
merchants.

Guildhall, the (London)
The historic building, built in 1411, that functions as the town hall
(and partly the local government building) of the City (of London).
It hosts official receptions and dinners in its banqueting hall, at
which important policy speeches are sometimes given by people
such as the Prime Minister and the Chancellor of the Exchequer.

Guillotine (government)
The parliamentary procedure in which debate on parts (or the
whole) of a bill that is passing through one of the Houses of
Parliament must be completed in one day. This allows the government to cut off debate to prevent delay in the passage of the bill.

Guilty (law)
The formal verdict delivered in a criminal court of law by magistrates or the jury against a person who has been found to have
committed an offence. The alternative verdict is Not Guilty. An
additional decision in Scotland is Not Proven.

Gutter press, the (media)
A common and critical term for popular newspapers and magazines
that dramatize and sensationalize current news events, such as disas-
ters and scandals. A gutter runs by the side of a pavement in the
street and collects rubbish and disposes of rain-water.

Guy Fawkes' Night (society)
An annual occasion (also known as Bonfire Night or the Fifth of November) on the evening of 5 November, which commemorates the Gunpowder Plot in 1605 when Roman Catholics (including Guy Fawkes) planned to kill King James I at the State Opening of Parliament by exploding barrels of gunpowder in the cellars of the Houses of Parliament. A bonfire on public or private land is set alight to burn a guy (a model of a human figure originally representing Guy Fawkes), and fireworks are set off.

Gymkhana (sport and leisure)
A sporting and social occasion, mainly for relatively affluent families, in which children and their horses take part in races and other contests.

H

Habeas corpus (law)
A legal demand from a judge, having its origin in ancient Habeas Corpus Acts, stipulating that an individual who is being kept in custody or prison must attend the court in order that the judge can decide whether or not that individual was lawfully imprisoned. A defence lawyer may apply to the court for such an order in the hope that a client will be released from custody while the case is further examined.

Hackney carriage (transport)
A term, originally describing a horse-drawn carriage, which is still applied to a taxi that has been licensed by local authorities throughout Britain (or by the Metropolitan Police in London) to carry fare-paying passengers.

Hadrian's Wall (geography)
See **English Heritage**.

Half-term (education)
The short (usually a week) holiday that state and independent schools give to their pupils half-way through a school term.

Hall of residence (education)
A residential building or hostel in many institutions of higher education, in which students live during term time and where conferences may be held in the vacations.

Hallé Orchestra, the (arts)
A well known symphony orchestra, established in Manchester in 1857, which is usually associated with, and tours, the north of England.

Hampden Park (sport and leisure)
A football stadium in Glasgow, Scotland (the counterpart to Wembley Stadium in London) where international football matches and the annual Scottish Cup Final (the counterpart of the English Cup Final) are played.

Hansard (government)
The common name for the daily report (formally called the Official

Report of Parliamentary Debates), first printed in 1774, that gives a verbatim (word-for-word) account of all proceedings and debates in the House of Commons.

Harefield Hospital (medicine)
A well known NHS hospital in West London that, together with Papworth Hospital near Cambridge, has successfully pioneered and specialized in heart transplant operations.

Harley Street (medicine)
The street in central London which is well known for its concentration of private medical specialists and consultants, and a name synonymous with private medicine in Britain.

Harrods (commerce)
A large, well known store in central London established in the 1840s, which is divided into many departments covering a very wide range of goods and services.

Harvest festival (religion)
An annual church service held usually on a Sunday in the autumn by Christian Churches, and especially the Church of England, to celebrate the successful completion of the agricultural season. Churches are traditionally decorated with fruit, vegetables, loaves of bread and other harvest produce.

Harwell (science)
The common name for the Atomic Energy Research Establishment in Oxfordshire, which is the central nuclear energy research and development organization of the United Kingdom Atomic Energy Authority (UKAEA).

Hat trick (sport and leisure)
A player who scores three goals in football and similar sports, or a bowler who dismisses three batsmen with successive balls in a cricket match, is said to have scored a hat trick. The term is also used in more general situations which involve a treble success.

H-blocks (law)
The central buildings of the Maze Prison, near Belfast, Northern Ireland, which are constructed in the shape of a letter H. The Maze is a high-security prison in which terrorist prisoners are (and suspects under internment were) kept.

Head of state (government)
The monarch is the head of state in Britain and the Prime Minister

is the head of government. The two functions are independent of each other.

Headmasters' Conference, the (HMC) (education)
An organization to which some 250 independent schools for boys belong, most of which are classified as public schools, and some of which have now become coeducational. It is an umbrella body for such schools and tries to represent their interests. The Girls' Public Day School Trust does a similar job for girls' independent schools. There are other bodies in addition to these, under various titles, which together represent some 550 of the most prominent independent schools.

Headteacher (education)
The person who is appointed to lead a school and who is responsible for its educational programmes, finance and administrative functions. The headteacher may still be known as a headmaster (male) or headmistress (female).

Health centre (Clinic) (medicine)
See **Group practice**.

Health visitor (medicine)
A professionally trained medical worker, employed usually by the local health authority, who provides medical care and health services for families with young children and babies, often in their homes but also in health centres. She is part of the local state health network and co-ordinates her work with other medical workers and doctors.

Heathrow (transport)
Britain's biggest international airport (formally called London Airport), west of London, which opened in 1946 and is connected to the capital by the Piccadilly line of the Underground. It is the world's busiest airport (in terms of daily aircraft movements) and handles scheduled and charter passenger flights, in addition to freight traffic.

Heavy goods vehicle (HGV) (transport)
A big commercial vehicle, which carries heavy cargo and for which the driver must have a special driving licence (an HGV licence) and pass a specialist driving test.

Henley (Royal) Regatta (sport and leisure)
A leading international rowing competition and socially fashionable

occasion, established in 1834. It is an annual event over five days in late June and early July on the River Thames at Henley, Oxfordshire. The Diamond Skulls for single oarsmen is one of its best known international races.

Her (His) Majesty (HM) (royalty)
The official title of, or reference for, the sovereign, as in Her (His) Majesty the Queen (the King).

Her (His) Majesty's Government (HMG) (government)
The formal name for the sitting government in Britain, which constitutionally acts on behalf of the sovereign.

Her (His) Majesty's Ship (HMS) (military)
The formal title of Royal Navy ships, given before the name of the ship, as in HMS *Ark Royal*, illustrating the fact that the monarch is the commander-in-chief of the armed forces.

Her (His) Majesty's Stationery Office (HMSO) (government)
The official government publisher, established in 1786. It publishes parliamentary documents (such as Green and White papers), material from government departments and other official bodies, and a range of informational books.

Heritage coast (geography)
One of the 44 undeveloped pieces of land around the British coastline which is officially defined by the Countryside Commission in England (and similar bodies in Wales and Scotland) as an area of scenic beauty and consequently protected under statute against commercial or industrial development.

High Church, the (religion)
The wing of the Church of England which emphasizes the historical connection between the Church and the Roman Catholic Church; the authority of the priesthood and clergy; the role of the sacraments; and the importance of ritual in worship.

High Court (of Justice), the (law)
The intermediate court in England and Wales between the county court and the Court of Appeal that deals with higher-level civil cases and some criminal ones. It comprises the three sections of the Chancery Division, the Queen's Bench Division and the Family Division. Each division is composed of High Court judges who usually sit alone (without a jury) when hearing a case. The central High Court is in London, but it has local branches in the main

English and Welsh cities. Northern Ireland also has a High Court
system while the equivalent in Scotland is the Court of Session.

High rise block (housing)
The multi-storeyed buildings consisting of flats (and also known as
tower blocks) which were erected mainly by local government councils in the 1960s to house urban populations displaced by slum
clearance programmes.

High school (education)
A term used historically for some ancient independent secondary
schools, which were mainly founded for the education of boys.
Today it is employed for some secondary schools for boys and
especially for many secondary schools for girls, both in the state
and independent sectors of school education.

High Street, the (society)
The official name of a central or main street in a town, city or
village, with shops, other commercial premises and offices. The
High Street was historically the most important, and in some cases
the only, street.

Higher education (HE) (education)
Education leading to a first or advanced degree at an institution of
higher education, such as a university, polytechnic or college (institute) of higher education, which is different from the further education sector.

Higher education funding councils (HEFC) (education)
Bodies made up of representatives from universities, polytechnics
and colleges (institutes) of higher education which during 1992–3
replaced existing structures. They allocate funds from central
government for teaching and research in higher education institutions which, although largely independent, are funded by public
money from general taxation. There are funding councils in Wales,
Scotland, England and Northern Ireland.

Highland Gathering (sport and leisure)
An annual celebration, also known as the Highland Games, of
Scottish sports and music held in the Highlands of Scotland. The
most famous is the Braemar Gathering, traditionally attended by
the royal family and established in 1832. Gatherings (or Games)
are also held at other centres, both in and outside the Highlands.
The sports activities include tossing the caber, wrestling and Scottish
country (or folk) dancing.

Highway Code, the (transport)
A booklet published by the government and first issued in 1931,
which contains traffic rules and regulations applicable to all road
users. The Green Cross Code is a junior set of traffic safety rules
for children which is circulated in the schools, first published in
1971.

Hire purchase (HP) agreement (finance)
A legal and financial arrangement between a purchaser and a commercial business, whereby the purchaser pays a deposit (of money)
and takes possession of goods under a hire agreement. The balance
of the purchase price for the goods plus an interest charge is then
paid by regular instalments over a fixed period of time. At the end
of the period, ownership of the goods passes to the purchaser.

Hogmanay (society)
The traditional term employed in Scotland for New Year's Eve (31
December), together with its festivities.

Holding company (finance)
A company, usually a main or parent organization, which, as part
of its total business empire, has (or holds) controlling shareholdings
in other companies, and can therefore influence the latters'
activities.

Home Counties, the (geography)
The Home Counties is a special term to describe those counties
which are in close proximity to London such as Essex, Kent and
Surrey. See also **Provinces**.

Home help (society)
An individual (now known as a community care assistant) employed
by the social services department of a local government authority
to provide mainly cleaning assistance in the home for those such
as the sick, the disabled and the elderly. A district nurse will supply
the medical aspects of such a service.

Home Office, the (HO) (government)
The government department which is in charge of internal domestic
matters in Britain, headed by the Home Secretary. It is mainly
concerned with law and order, immigration, public meetings, and
race and community relations.

Home rule (politics)
A term which is still used today, particularly in connection with

independence and devolution proposals for Scotland and Wales. Historically it is associated with unsuccessful campaigns by Irish nationalists in the late nineteenth and early twentieth centuries who called for the self-government of Ireland, free from English control. After the establishment of Northern Ireland from 1921 and eventually the Republic of Ireland, the campaign for Irish unification was continued by Sinn Fein and the IRA.

Home Secretary, the (government)
The secretary of state who is the government minister in charge of the Home Office and therefore internal and security matters in Britain, together with the secretaries of state for Scotland, Wales and Northern Ireland.

Honours system, the (society)
The awarding of honorary titles, such as orders like the Order of the British Empire (OBE), life peerages, medals like the British Empire Medal (BEM), and knighthoods to people in Britain and sometimes overseas. It is mainly organized in the name of the sovereign by the Prime Minister and government, although the monarch and the government can issue their own independent lists of honours. Honours are generally awarded in the New Year, on the sovereign's Official Birthday (currently the second Saturday in June) and following a dissolution of Parliament. The Conservative government intends to democratize and reform the system.

Horse of the Year Show, the (sport and leisure)
A show-jumping contest to determine the most successful show-jumpers and their horses each year in October. It was first organized in 1949 and is now held normally at a London venue such as Wembley Arena or Earls Court.

Hospice (medicine)
A residential nursing home or clinic, usually privately financed and organized, which cares for the terminally ill. An increasing number have been founded in Britain in recent years.

House (education)
Traditionally a separate building in a boarding or public school where a specific group of pupils lives, and which is distinguished by a name or title. A school may have several houses whose members have a particular identity in internal school competitions, such as sporting contests. The term is also used for the same purpose in some state schools.

House of Commons, the (HC) (government)
The lower, but politically most significant, branch of the British
Parliament, which comprises 651 elected MPs: 524 for England, 38
for Wales, 72 for Scotland and 17 for Northern Ireland. The principal functions of the House are to make national law by passing
Acts of Parliament, authorize government expenditure, scrutinize
government policies and debate current political issues. It sits for
five days a week for much of the year, and has a maximum legal
term of five years, at the end of which a general election should
normally be called.

House of Lords, the (HL) (government)
The upper, less politically significant, branch of the British Parliament, which comprises some 1,200 non-elected members or peers
(Lords Spiritual and Lords Temporal), of whom about 300 attend
regularly. It acts as a revising body, examines bills which are sent
from the Commons, discusses a range of matters for which the
Commons lacks time, proposes amendments to bills, oversees European Community legislation, serves as a final court of appeal for
most parts of Britain, and normally sits for four days a week for a
little over half a year.

Household Cavalry (Troops), the (military)
A branch of the British Army, consisting of two cavalry regiments,
that performs special ceremonial and guard functions for the sovereign, in addition to conventional military duties. Together with the
infantry regiments of the Guards Division they are known as the
Household (or Royal) Troops, and all take part in the annual
Trooping the Colour on Horse Guards Parade in London on the
sovereign's Official Birthday.

Housemaster/mistress (education)
The teacher who is responsible for the organization of a house
principally in a boys' or girls' boarding school, but also in other
schools.

Houses of Parliament, the (government)
The buildings in London beside the River Thames which contain
the House of Commons and the House of Lords and where politicians debate and decide parliamentary business. The site was originally developed for national government in the fourteenth century
and the buildings have been frequently rebuilt and developed over
the centuries.

Housing associations (housing)
Independent organizations which operate at the local level throughout Britain, and which may receive government finance. They reno-
vate old property, build new homes and provide rented houses and
flats for low-income families, the elderly, the disabled and single
people.

Housing benefit (finance)
A state benefit within the social security system which is paid to
employed and unemployed people on low incomes to help them
pay their rent and housing costs. The amount is dependent upon
family status and total income.

Housing Corporation, the (housing)
A statutory body in England which supervises and allocates grants
to housing associations, and protects the rights of housing association tenants. The grants of state finance to private organizations
are intended to increase the number of houses and flats available
on the housing market. Similar bodies perform the same functions
in Wales, Scotland and Northern Ireland.

Housing estate (housing)
A specially designed area of public or private housing in a city or
on its outskirts, which usually has its own shops, restaurants, pubs,
churches and health centres.

Hovercraft (transport)
A vehicle specially designed to travel over land or sea on a cushion
of air. It is used by the Hoverspeed company Sealink which operates
regular cross-Channel passenger services from Hoverports on the
English south-east coast.

Hung parliament (government and politics)
The situation which may arise in the British parliamentary electoral
system when, after a general election, no one party has achieved
an overall majority of the seats in the House of Commons. This
means that the party with the largest number of seats may form a
minority government (with the danger of being out-voted by the
opposition parties), or can enter into a pact by which a small
opposition party agrees to support it, or it can form a coalition
government with an opposition party.

Hunt (sport and leisure)
An organization of men and women who usually hunt wild animals
on horseback or sometimes on foot, and are led by a Master of

Foxhounds (MFH) or Hounds. Traditional hunts, such as the Quorn, hunt foxes on horseback with hounds (or dogs). They have a base in a particular county or area of the countryside and their members wear distinctively coloured clothes. Hunting is a sport associated mainly with country people, landowners and farmers, and has in recent years come increasingly under attack from movements such as the League Against Cruel Sports and other animals' rights organizations.

Hyde Park (London)
See **Royal salute** and **Speakers' Corner**.

Hymns Ancient and Modern (Hymns A and M) (religion)
The semi-official book of hymns, first published in 1861, which is used at church services in the Church of England. It contains many standard and well known hymns which are also employed in other contexts outside church services and by other denominations.

I

Immigration Acts (government)
The series of Acts of Parliament and accompanying Immigration Rules and regulations passed since the nineteenth century, and particularly in the 1960s and 1970s (such as the Immigration Acts of 1968 and 1971) by both Conservative and Labour governments, which have collectively reduced the number of immigrants entering Britain, and strengthened the rules against entry.

Imprisonment (law)
The procedure by which an individual accused and found guilty of certain criminal offences may be sentenced by the court to a period of detention (a custodial sentence) in a prison for varying lengths of time. The precise number of months/years involved will depend on the court, the nature of the offence and the punishment prescribed by statute.

Income (finance)
Although there is no legal definition of income in Britain, it refers generally to money and other financial benefits which an individual receives, normally as a result of paid employment and investments. The term is also applied to the finance that groups, companies and governments receive.

Income Support (finance)
The means-tested basic benefit within the state social security system, which is paid in variable amounts to individuals who lack enough money to provide for their needs, like the unemployed, some old age pensioners (OAPs), single parents, the sick and the disabled.

Income tax (IT) (finance)
A direct state tax which is charged on the money an individual earns from employment and/or receives from investments in a tax year (from 6 April to 5 April the following year). It is assessed on total income less specific deductions and allowances. At present the rate of tax is 20 per cent on the lowest bands of income and then 25 per cent up to the first £23,700 earned (the basic rate), with 40 per cent on higher earnings. Income tax is assessed and collected

by local branches of a government department, the Inland Revenue (IR).

Incumbent (religion and society)
Generally can refer to anyone who holds a particular position of authority or status. In religious terms this usually means a priest or other member of the clergy.

Independent (politics)
An elected politician, either at local or central government level, who is not a member of one of the political parties in Britain. There were more Independents in the past than at present and there are still some in local government and the House of Lords. But the growth of organized political parties has reduced their numbers.

Independent education (education)
The term used to distinguish the private (or non-state) sector of British education (comprising fee-paying schools and other institutions) from the state or public sector.

Independent Local Radio (ILR) (media)
The Radio Authority (formed in 1991) awards licences to and supervises the programmes and services of the private companies that operate independent local radio stations throughout Britain, and which are largely financed by advertising revenue. The first commercial stations were established in 1973, since when their numbers have increased to some 79.

Independent nuclear deterrent (military)
Britain's independent nuclear force which in the mid-1990s will consist mainly of four Trident missile-armed submarines (replacing Polaris missiles) operated by the Royal Navy, but also including various types of land-based and air-to-ground missiles.

Independent Radio News (IRN) (media)
An independent national and international news service supplied by the London Broadcasting Company (LBC) to local independent radio stations licensed and supervised by the Radio Authority.

Independent schools (education)
Private, fee-paying schools at both primary and secondary levels (comprising preparatory, public and other independent schools) that are separate from the state school system. Some are ancient foundations while others are relatively new. They generally have a high

reputation for their academic standards, but only some 7.5 per cent of all British schoolchildren in the relevant age groups attend independent schools.

Independent Television (ITV) (media)
An independent television channel (ITV) which is supervised by the ITC and also known as Channel 3 from 1993. It broadcasts programmes for some 24 hours daily made by the 15 production companies (such as Yorkshire and Central) which are licensed by the ITC (with 10-year licences from 1993), and which supply the 14 regions into which Britain is divided for ITV/Channel 3 purposes.

Independent Television Commission (ITC) (media)
The body (replacing the Independent Broadcasting Authority [IBA]) established in 1990 to license and supervise the non-BBC independent (or commercial) television services, which currently are Channel 3 (also known as ITV), Channel 4, the proposed Channel 5, and cable, teletext and satellite services.

Independent Television News (ITN) (media)
An independent company that supplies a 24-hours-a-day news service for Channel 4 and the 15 ITC-supervised regional pro-gramme companies of Channel 3 (also known as ITV), which at present are all shareholders in ITN. The main ITN news pro-grammes are at midday and in the early and late evening.

Indictable (law)
The category of serious criminal offences, such as murder, major theft and rape, which can only be tried before a judge and jury in the crown court and not by a magistrates' court.

Individual responsibility of ministers (government)
See **Ministerial responsibility**.

Industrial action (employment)
An active industrial protest or dispute, like a strike, go-slow or work-to-rule in a factory or place of employment, where there is conflict between employers (or management) and employees usually over pay or conditions of work.

Industrial estate (commerce and industry)
A specially designated area usually on the outskirts of a town or city (frequently a New Town) which comprises factories, service facilities and the premises of commercial firms.

Industrial relations (employment and industry)
The work relationship between employers, management and employees, in which both the trade unions (including the Trades Union Congress [TUC]) and the Confederation of British Industry (CBI) are involved. British industrial relations have often been regarded as too confrontational and too much tied to class-war images of us-and-them. The Advisory, Conciliation and Arbitration Service (ACAS) frequently plays a leading role in trying to mediate between the opposing sides.

Infant (law)
An individual in Britain legally remains an infant until the age of 18 and is subject until then to restrictions, such as the inability to own land or to make a valid will.

Infant school (education)
A state primary school for young children from the start of compulsory education at the age of 5 up to 7, after which they usually enter a junior school from 7 to 11. The two schools may be in the same, or separate, buildings.

Inheritance tax (IHT) (finance)
The direct state tax which is levied on money and property left to individuals in a will by a deceased person, and potentially on other transfers of assets and finance from one individual to another during a testator's lifetime. There are some specific exemptions from IHT and no tax is currently charged on amounts of less than £150,000.

Inherited wealth (finance)
A common term to describe money and property which is left to a descendant of a deceased person, usually by will, and which is not earned income.

Inland Revenue (Board of), the (IR) (government)
The government department that applies and supervises the tax laws in Britain, and whose regional offices are in charge of assessing and collecting income tax from individuals and corporation tax from companies.

Inn (society)
A term for an establishment which historically provided accommodation and refreshment for road travellers, and today is another name for a public house (pub) or small hotel (which may be very old). It is often incorporated in the name of the property, such as

the Ship Inn or the Market Inn, which is displayed on an illustrated inn sign outside the premises.

Inner Cabinet (government)
The small group of advisers and confidantes around a Prime Minister who, together with the Prime Minister, may often be responsible for the creation of government policy outside the Cabinet proper.

Inner city (geography)
An area of many big British cities and towns that is near to or in the business and shopping centre. It may be characterized by high unemployment, social problems, a shifting population, economic decline, a high crime rate and decaying or derelict property. In the early 1990s the Conservative government began attempts to improve inner-city conditions through rebuilding programmes and action schemes to provide employment and business opportunities.

Inner London (geography)
A term used to describe the 12 central boroughs and inner districts of London, which fall within the larger area of Greater London.

Inns of Court, the (law)
The four legal associations (Lincoln's Inn, Inner Temple, Middle Temple and Gray's Inn) and their medieval properties in central London, to one of which all barristers and judges must belong. The Inns contain chambers (from which some 2,000 barristers practise), administrative offices, libraries, eating halls, lawyers' flats and solicitors' firms.

Inquest (law)
An inquiry or investigation by a coroner (and his or her office) in England and Wales (or a procurator-fiscal in Scotland) into the cause of a person's death in a local area, particularly if the death is sudden or there are suspicious circumstances. The coroner may be assisted by a jury in some cases.

Institute of Directors, the (ID) (employment)
A nationwide and influential association of businessmen established in 1903 which, together with the Confederation of British Industry (CBI) and similar groups, represents the interests of businesses mostly in the private sector of the economy.

Insurance broker (finance)
A private financial agent who selects and organizes different types of insurance (a guarantee against loss) on behalf of other people and who is paid by commission or fee.

Inter-City train (transport)
A fast passenger train of British Rail (BR) that operates on main-line railway routes between major cities, such as London–Birmingham or Newcastle–Edinburgh. Some of the trains are commonly known as Inter-City 125s since they are capable of travelling at 125 miles an hour (201 km an hour). Faster trains have recently been introduced on some major lines, particularly in eastern England.

Interest rates (finance)
The additional amount or charge (assessed in percentage terms) that a borrower must pay to a lender, such as a building society or bank, when repaying the capital on a loan (for example, 10 per cent per year on a loan of £10,000). Interest rates vary among financial institutions and may go up or down over time.

Internment (law)
The former British government practice (which stopped in 1975) of imprisoning suspected (and unconvicted) persons in Northern Ireland (mainly in the Maze Prison) in order to curb terrorist activities.

Invalidity benefit (finance)
The state benefit (currently £54 per week) in the social security system which is paid to people who are off work due to illness for more than 28 weeks and when other sickness benefits end. If an individual is ill for less than the 28 weeks, he or she can claim statutory sick pay (up to £52 per week) from an employer, or the state sickness benefit (£41.20 per week) if he or she is unable to claim the statutory sick pay.

Investigative journalism (media)
A particular form of journalism which carries out detailed, in-depth inquiries into various aspects of social, political and economic life, often with the intention of exposing the truth about a particular matter.

Investment trust (finance)
A private financial company that invests money deposited with it by shareholders, and pays them a dividend out of any eventual income or profits that it receives from its investments.

Invisible exports (commerce and finance)
Earnings from British exports such as shipping, tourism, insurance and aviation charges which are not calculated in the normal national balance of payments equation, but which in practice add appreciably

to the total value of exports, and help to reduce a potential trade deficit.

Ireland (geography)
The second-largest and most westerly island of the British Isles, separated from Great Britain (Wales, Scotland and England) by St George's Channel and the Irish Sea. The term Ireland can refer geographically to the whole island (and for Irish nationalists to a constitutional unit encompassing both North and South). But it is usually employed (at least in Britain) to indicate the Republic of Ireland (Eire) as distinct from Northern Ireland (which is part of the United Kingdom).

Irish Republican Army (Provisional), the (IRA) (politics)
An organization of militant Irish nationalists, known as the Provisionals, which split from the Official IRA in 1969–70. They have a following among Catholics, and their campaigns of violence in Northern Ireland and on the mainland of Britain are intended to lead to a united Irish Republic (consisting of Eire and Northern Ireland). The Provisionals are illegal in Britain and the Irish Republic, but are supported by a legal political wing (Sinn Fein).

Isle of Man, the (geography and government)
See **Crown dependency**.

J

Jobber (finance)
See **Big Bang** and **Stockbroker**.

Jobcentre (government and employment)
An office or shop in towns and cities throughout Britain, provided and serviced by local government authorities, where job advertisements and employment opportunities are displayed and where an individual needing employment advice can be helped by specialist advisers. Various other services may also be available such as help in drafting applications to prospective employers.

Jockey Club, the (JC) (sport and leisure)
The independent governing body of British horse-racing, established in 1750, which is responsible for all race meetings (on the flat and steeplechasing) and the supervision of horses, owners, trainers and officials in the sport.

John o' Groats (geography)
A village situated at the north-east tip of Scotland, which has been traditionally thought of as the most northerly point of mainland Britain and is contrasted to Land's End at the south-western tip of England. The two places are some 600 miles (965 km) apart.

Judicial Committee (of the Privy Council), the (law)
The influential judicial section of the Privy Council in London which serves as the final court of appeal in criminal and some civil matters from those dependencies and Commonwealth countries which have retained this avenue of appeal from colonial days. It may also be used to decide cases for a wide range of courts and committees in Britain and overseas.

Judiciary, the (law)
The third branch of the constitutional division of powers in Britain together with the legislature and the executive. It is mainly composed of the senior judges in the higher courts and is independent of and subordinate to the other two branches. The judges apply the law (including the common law) and interpret Acts of Parliament.

Junior school (education)
See **Infant school**.

Jurisdiction (law and society)
A term which describes both the professional and geographical competence of an organization, such as a magistrates' court which has a limited legal power and is restricted to a local area. It is also used in other social, legal and political contexts to indicate a defined area of authority.

Jury (law)
The 12 citizens (known as jurors) who are selected to give a verdict (guilty or not guilty) according to the evidence which is presented in a criminal case in the crown court in England and Wales. Their decision is usually unanimous, but they are allowed to give a majority verdict, provided that there are not more than two dissenters, that is, 10–2. If a decision is not reached, there must be a retrial. Juries may also be used in certain civil cases, such as those dealing with libel (or defamation of character), and they also serve in Scotland and Northern Ireland in both criminal and civil matters.

Justice of the Peace (law)
See **Magistrate**.

Juvenile court (law)
A court of law in Northern Ireland (now a youth court in England and Wales and a children's panel in Scotland) that determines cases in which young people from 10 to 17 years of age are charged with a criminal offence.

K

Kew Gardens (London)
An area of parkland, greenhouses containing exotic plants and flowers, and elegant buildings which is open to the public and situated near the River Thames at Kew in Surrey, south-west of London. It is also a centre for botanical research, known officially as the Royal Botanic Gardens. Most sections of the Public Record Office (which holds national and government documents) are now situated near Kew Gardens.

Kindergarten (education)
Another name for a nursery school, particularly a private one, normally for children below the age of 5.

King's counsel (KC) (law)
See **Queen's counsel**.

Kirk, the (religion)
The term often used for a church building of the Church of Scotland, and an expression frequently employed to describe the Church itself as a distinctive denomination.

L

Labour market, the (employment)
The term used for the number and types of people available for work nationally. It is related to other terms such as 'labour costs' (the amount of money needed to employ the workforce in specific areas of production), and 'labour-intensive' (meaning that some industries require greater numbers of workers because of the nature of the job, in contrast to high-technology or professional work which needs less).

Labour Party, the (politics)
The biggest left-wing political party and alternative to the Conservatives in Britain. Historically it has campaigned on behalf of the labour or working class against the employers and capital-owners. It developed towards the end of the nineteenth century under various titles, and was officially named and established as the Labour Party in 1906. It is supported mainly by working people in the urban and industrialized areas of the Midlands and north of England, mid-Scotland and South Wales, together with some middle-class followers. It is closely associated with the trade union movement, from which it receives financial aid.

Lady-in-waiting (royalty)
Normally a female from the gentry or aristocracy, who serves the sovereign or other members of the royal family in a personal capacity.

Laird (society)
The ancient title of a landowner in Scotland, who often has an influential status and role in the local community.

Lambeth Conference, the (religion)
A meeting of bishops of the worldwide Anglican Communion (including the Church of England), presided over by the Archbishop of Canterbury, which has taken place every 10 years since 1867 at Lambeth Palace (the official South London residence of the Archbishop of Canterbury). The Conference may produce influential reports on social, political and religious matters.

Landlady/landlord (housing and commerce)
A landlady is a woman who owns domestic property (such as a boarding house, lodgings, house, bedsitter or flat), and rents it out to tenants. A landlord is a man in a similar position, but who may also own and rent out commercial premises. A company owning and renting property is legally known as a landlord. The person in charge of a public house (a pub) is also known as a landlady/landlord.

Land's End (geography)
The south-west tip of mainland England, in Cornwall, which is frequently used in contrast to John o' Groats in the far north of Scotland, with the distance between them being some 600 miles (965 km).

Landslide victory (politics)
An election result which produces a substantially increased number of votes (and consequently a greater majority) for one party at the expense of another (or others).

Law centre (law)
An office (also known as a legal centre) staffed by lawyers and other professionals (such as social workers), often in a deprived urban location, which is financed by local or central government and which provides free legal advice for those in need.

Law Courts, the (law and London)
A common name for the Gothic-style court buildings in the Strand, London, which house the Court of Appeal and the central premises of the High Court.

Law lords, the (law)
Specialist legal peers in the House of Lords who function as the highest court of appeal for civil cases in Britain and for criminal cases in England, Wales and Northern Ireland. They comprise those peers who have held senior judicial office in the court system and may be presided over on occasions by the Lord Chancellor. Normally 3–4 will sit to decide an appeal case.

Law Society, the (LS) (law)
The statutory organization in central London (but with local branches throughout England and Wales), founded in 1825, which serves as a professional association for most solicitors. It grants practising certificates to solicitors, investigates complaints about

their conduct and organizes the education and training of student solicitors.

Lawyer (law)
A general name for both solicitors and barristers in England and Wales, and for members of the legal profession elsewhere in Britain.

Layman (society)
An ordinary citizen who is not a professionally qualified expert in a particular field such as the law or religion, but who may feel free to comment (for example) on legal and religious matters in a general sense.

Lay reader (preacher) (religion)
An individual who is not a professional or ordained member of a church, but who is permitted to conduct a limited range of religious services and to give Bible readings.

L-driver (transport)
An individual, also known as a learner-driver, who is learning to drive a vehicle such as a car or motor-cycle on the road with a provisional licence, and whose vehicle carries L-plates (a red letter L on a white background), to distinguish it from other traffic on the road.

Leader of the House, the (government)
A senior MP in the House of Commons from the government party who has managerial responsibility for organizing the daily business of the House and the implementation of the government's legislative plans. The job is often combined with that of Lord President of the Council and is frequently given cabinet rank. A similar position with the same functions is held by a peer in the House of Lords, who is the spokesperson for the government there.

Leader of the (Official) Opposition, the (government)
The elected leader of the largest opposition party in the House of Commons. That party is the Official Opposition (known formally as Her Majesty's Loyal Opposition) to the government and, if it wins the next general election, its leader will normally become Prime Minister.

Leading article (media)
See **Articles** and **Editorials**.

League Against Cruel Sports, the (sport and leisure)
See **Hunt** and **Blood sports**.

Leave to appeal (law)
The permission given by a court, after a case has been heard and
decided, which enables a dissatisfied party to appeal to the next
higher court. Sometimes the appeal can be against both the decision
and the sentence, in other cases only against sentence. At the
higher levels leave to appeal must be granted first by the Court of
Appeal, then by the House of Lords.

Lecturer (education)
The name and position of a teacher in further and higher education,
ranking below that of professor, who gives a course of lectures to
students.

Left of centre/left wing (politics)
In Britain, left of centre identifies parties like the Liberal Democrats
and left wing describes political parties such as the Labour Party,
in order to distinguish them from right-wing or right-of-centre
parties such as the Conservatives. Such terms are also used to
describe different groupings within parties.

Legal aid (law)
A state system, established in 1949, whereby those people who are
unable to afford legal advice and representation in criminal and
civil matters because of their low income may have their legal bills
paid by the state if they have a suitable case. They are sometimes
required to repay the legal aid, depending on whether the court
awards them money or property as a result of their case.

Legislation (law)
The term to describe both the law-making (legislative) process in
itself and the eventual law (or Act) which results from the process.

Legislature, the (law and government)
The supreme law-creating body in Britain (except for some legislation deriving from superior European Community institutions)
which consists collectively of the House of Lords, the House of
Commons and the monarch. It constitutes one of the three branches
in the division of powers, the others being the executive and the
judiciary.

Lent (religion)
The period of penitence for Christians in Britain during which

people traditionally fasted or abstained from particular foods, such as meat and eggs, in the past. It continues for 40 days from Ash Wednesday until the Saturday before Easter Sunday.

Libel (law)
The making of written or published accusations by one person against another which are proved in the High Court to be false or harmful to an individual's reputation, and for which damages may be awarded.

Liberty (law)
Formerly the National Council for Civil Liberties (NCCL), established in 1934, which changed its name in 1991. It is a voluntary organization which defends and furthers the civil liberties and rights of individual citizens, and fights discrimination and the abuse of power.

Licensing hours (society)
The daily times when public houses (pubs) may legally open for the public sale of alcoholic drinks. The hours used to vary considerably throughout Britain, but were generally from 11.30 am to 2.30 pm and 6.00 pm to 10.30 pm. From 1988, however, pubs have been permitted to stay open from 11.00 am to 11.00 pm if they so choose, although some keep to the old hours.

Life imprisonment (law)
See **Capital punishment**.

Life peers (politics and government)
Individuals, usually retired politicians and trade unionists but also businessmen, academics and others, who have been suggested by political parties to sit in the House of Lords and who are created peers for their lifetime. They can represent a particular party or be Independents, and may be awarded the title because of past services or because a political party wants them to be working members of the Lords.

Listed building (government)
A property which has been officially designated as being of architectural or historic importance. It is protected under statute and cannot be destroyed or altered without permission from a local government authority.

Litigation (law)
The administrative process through which a legal action passes from

start to finish, and which will often conclude with the case being heard in court.

Lloyd's (finance)
An insurance market comprising private associations of London underwriters (groups of insurers willing to bear any eventual loss), founded in 1688. Historically it dealt mainly with marine, shipping and trading insurance, and still publishes a daily record (*Lloyd's List*) of shipping information. Today it also handles a wide range of other insurance policies.

Lloyd's Bank (finance)
One of the five leading English banks, established in 1865, and with branches in towns and cities throughout Britain, which provide banking and financial services to individual and commercial customers.

Lloyd's Register (LR) (transport)
A private society established in 1760 to identify and categorize merchant ships on a world basis. Today it still publishes a *Register* giving details of all sea-going vessels.

Lobby/lobbyist (politics and society)
An organization or group of people which brings pressure to bear, usually on government departments, in order to have some sectional interest achieved, such as tobacco companies lobbying Parliament to reduce taxes on cigarettes.

Local authority (government)
A governmental and political organization, in the form of a council, elected by local electorates throughout Britain which organizes the municipal services of an area such as a district or county.

Local education authority (LEA) (education)
The local government organization in a county in England and Wales that supervises and determines educational policy and services in most of the state schools and (formerly) colleges of further education in its area. It hires teachers, maintains and repairs school property, provides educational equipment and supervises the school curriculum.

Local enterprise company (LEC) (employment)
See **Employment Training**.

Local government (government)
The system of local authorities or elected councils based on coun-

ties, districts, boroughs and regions which organizes local municipal services throughout Britain, and is distinguished from the work of central government in London.

Local management of schools, the (LMS) (education)
Recent Conservative government reforms in state schools have given headteachers a greater amount of administrative responsibility, both educational and financial, for the organization of their individual schools. They have now taken over some (but not all) of the previous educational functions of local government.

Local radio (media)
A general term for radio stations operated both by the BBC and the independent Radio Authority, which provide services for a local area such as a city and its immediate surroundings. They supply information of local interest, news bulletins, programmes of light or popular music, and phone-ins by the general public. The BBC has some 37 local radio stations in England and the Channel Islands (in addition to others in Scotland, Wales and Northern Ireland), while the Radio Authority has some 79 stations in Britain as a whole.

Lockout (employment)
The physical closing of a workplace, such as a factory or an office, by an employer during an industrial dispute, so that the workforce cannot enter the premises. This may be done to pressurize the employees into accepting the employer's terms for settling the dispute.

Lombard Street (finance)
A street in the City (of London) so-called because financiers from Lombardy, Italy, carried on business there in the medieval period. The name has been historically identified with banking and the London financial markets.

London (London)
Situated on the banks of the River Thames, London is Britain's capital and its largest city, with a population of some 6.4 million. For local government purposes, London is administered by 32 borough councils and the independent City (of London). It contains the Houses of Parliament, central government departments and the Queen's primary residence (Buckingham Palace). The redeveloped London Docklands are in the East End; the West End is well known for its cinemas, theatres and shops; and the City (of London)

is a leading world financial centre. London has many interesting buildings, art galleries, concert halls and opera houses, and a number of large public parks.

London Docklands, the (London)
A recent redevelopment in the East End of London, following the closure of the last docks in the early 1980s and the transfer of shipping facilities to Tilbury, some 26 miles east of London. The former docks have now become a residential and commercial area, with new buildings erected to house financial and other professional concerns, and communications are provided by a light railway and an airport. But the economic recession from 1988 to 1992 has created financial problems for property developers and financiers, and some of the development is incomplete and properties unoccupied.

London Gazette, the (LG) (government)
An official journal, first published in 1665 and now issued four times a week by the government. It contains official announcements, legal advertisements, armed forces promotions, and the New Year, Dissolution and Birthday Honours lists.

London Library, the (LL) (arts)
Britain's biggest private lending library, in central London, consisting of members who have subscribed to its services. It was established in 1841 and currently contains some one million books on most humanities subjects. It is an important literary and historical institution with an expanding number of books and a possible building extension in the near future.

London Marathon, the (sport and leisure)
A 26-mile (42-km) road race held in London each year, in association with the British Athletics Federation (BAF). The commercially sponsored Marathon was first held in 1981 and its course runs through East, South and central London. The race attracts all types of runners, including international competitors, and may be used as a sponsored run to raise money for charity.

London Philharmonic Orchestra, the (LPO) (arts)
One of Britain's main symphony orchestras, founded in 1932, and now permanently based at the Royal Festival Hall, on the South Bank in London.

London Regional Transport (LRT) (transport)
The state organization (known commonly as London Transport)

which organizes public transport in the Greater London area through its three main companies, London Underground Ltd, London Buses Ltd and Docklands Light Railway Ltd.

Long vacation, the (education and law)
The annual summer holiday at an institution of higher education and in the law courts, which is normally for three months, from July to September.

Lord (government, religion and law)
1. A peer who is a member of the House of Lords, whether holding a life or hereditary title. 2. The formal title of a bishop in the Church of England. 3. The formal title of many senior judges.

Lord Advocate, the (government and law)
See **Attorney-General**.

Lord Chamberlain, the (royalty)
The chief administrative official and manager of the royal household, who also organizes some royal and public ceremonies.

Lord (High) Chancellor, the (government)
The chief legal officer in England and Wales, appointed by the sitting government. He is a member of the Cabinet and the Privy Council; the Speaker of the House of Lords (where he conducts proceedings from the woolsack); and head of the higher court system in England and Wales. Many of his legal duties are conducted through the Lord Chancellor's Department, a government legal department staffed by lawyers and civil servants.

Lord Chief Justice, the (LCJ) (law)
The senior judge who organizes the Queen's Bench Division in the High Court of Justice in England and Wales. He ranks second after the Lord Chancellor in the legal hierarchy, sits in the House of Lords as a peer, and is effectively the head of the criminal law system in England and Wales because he presides over the Criminal Division of the Court of Appeal.

Lord Lieutenant, the (government)
The honorary representative of the sovereign in a county in England and Wales, who can be male or female. The office dates from the sixteenth century, and was historically an influential position with many duties and responsibilities. Today it is largely ceremonial, although the Lord Lieutenant does recommend the appointment of Justices of the Peace (JPs).

Lord Mayor, the (LM) (government)
The title of the leading public official of the City (of London) and
of some other large cities in Britain (except Scotland), which may
be held by a man or a woman.

Lord Mayor's Banquet, the (London)
Following the annual election of a new Lord Mayor of London, a
dinner is held in the Guildhall, London, to which prominent British
and (often) overseas guests are invited. The Prime Minister usually
delivers an influential speech on some aspect of current government
policy.

Lord Mayor's Show, the (London)
An annual ceremony in November, when the newly elected Lord
Mayor of London rides in a horse-drawn carriage through the
streets of the City of London, followed by a procession of other
vehicles which are decorated according to a particular theme of the
new Lord Mayor's choice.

Lord President of the Council, the (LPC) (government)
The senior government minister, usually a member of the Cabinet,
who conducts the meetings of the Privy Council, organizes the
work of the Privy Council office, forwards items of business to the
sovereign, and may also be Leader either of the House of Commons
or House of Lords.

Lord Privy Seal, the (LPS) (government)
A senior member of the Cabinet who does not have any special
departmental or ministerial duties. He is often a peer and Leader
of the House of Lords, where he manages the business of the
House on behalf of the government.

Lord Provost, the (LP) (government)
The formal name of the leading public official of five Scottish cities:
Aberdeen, Dundee, Edinburgh, Glasgow and Perth. The position
is similar to that of a lord mayor in England.

Lord's (sport and leisure)
A well known cricket ground in North London. It is the headquarters of the Marylebone Cricket Club (MCC) (formerly the
ruling body of cricket), the home ground of Middlesex County
Cricket Club, and generally regarded as the home of world cricket.

Lord's Day Observance Society, the (LDOS) (society)
A voluntary organization established in 1831 to campaign for the

strict keeping of Sunday (the Christian Sabbath) as a day of rest and religious observance. The society opposes any legislation and activities that would allow commercial or sporting activities on Sundays.

Lords Justices of Appeal (law)
The judges who sit and decide cases (criminal and civil) in the Court of Appeal in England and Wales. They are appointed by the Crown on the advice of the Prime Minister and the Master of the Rolls. Similar judges perform the same role in the appeal courts in Scotland and Northern Ireland.

Lords Spiritual, the (government)
The term for the two archbishops and 24 senior bishops of the Church of England who are members of the House of Lords, and who represent the Church in its parliamentary connection.

Lords Temporal, the (government)
The term for all peers (hereditary, life and legal peers) in the House of Lords who are not counted as Lords Spiritual (or representative senior clergy of the Church of England).

Low Church (religion)
The wing of the Church of England which has been influenced by the evangelistic Christian tradition and, to some extent, by nonconformity. Unlike the High Church wing it stresses simple methods of worship and a lack of ritual in its services.

Lower middle class (society)
The social class of British society that occupies a half-way position between working class and upper middle class, and which usually consists of people such as clerical workers, shopkeepers and minor civil servants.

Lower school (education)
A name sometimes used for the junior classes of a secondary school in both the state and independent sectors of education. These classes may be organized as a middle school in the state comprehensive system.

Loyalists, the (politics)
Those Protestants in Northern Ireland who insist that Ulster should maintain its constitutional connection (union) with Britain, and who remain loyal to the British Crown.

M

Magistrate (law)
A judicial official without professional legal qualifications, also known as a Justice of the Peace (JP), who is appointed by the Lord Chancellor. He or she sits in an unpaid and part-time capacity as a judge in local magistrates' courts in England, Wales and Northern Ireland to decide minor (summary) criminal and some civil cases without a jury.

Magistrates' court (law)
The lowest criminal court in England and Wales in which the majority of all crimes (95 per cent), but chiefly minor or summary cases, are heard and decided by a bench of local magistrates without a jury. It can also determine some civil cases, such as those dealing with marriage, divorce, licensing and motoring. There are magistrates' courts in Northern Ireland and sheriff/district courts in Scotland which perform the same duties.

Magna Carta (government)
See **Runnymede**.

Maiden speech (government)
The first or opening speech delivered by an MP in the House of Commons, or by a peer in the House of Lords, after he or she has become a member of the relevant House, and which is usually on a topic of personal interest to that individual.

Maintenance (law)
The amount of money ordered by a court of law to be paid by an ex-husband or wife to the other spouse and any children of the family after a divorce. Also occurs within marriage or on separation.

Maisonette (housing)
A small house, or part of a house let separately, which consists of a basic minimum of rooms and amenities.

Majority (government and politics)
In a general election, an ordinary majority is the number of popular votes that one party or candidate has over other parties or candidates (which can be a simple majority of one), both nationwide

and in the constituency, and which is converted into parliamentary seats. An overall (or absolute) majority is the popular vote translated into the number of seats in the House of Commons which the government has over all the other opposition parties counted together. The term is also employed in general meetings and other elections to signify the number of votes which one candidate (or proposal) has over competing ones.

Management (employment and commerce)
Those people, known as managers, who are in charge of and who organize (or manage) a particular factory, office or company. Often used in contrast to the workers (workforce or labour force) who put management decisions into effect.

Managing director (commerce)
In a company which is run by a board of directors, the managing director, who is often chosen by the other directors, is the executive leader of the board and frequently the initiator of ideas and policies.

Mandate (politics and government)
The British political theory (which still has some weight) that a government, once elected, has the right (is mandated) to carry out the political programmes or policies on which it was elected and which were included in its election manifesto.

Manifesto (politics)
The document (containing policy information) which a political party presents to the electorate in an election, and on which it hopes to gain power.

Manual worker (employment)
A social and employment classification describing workers who generally have no special skills and who work with their hands in a variety of unskilled jobs. But it can also sometimes be applied to semi-skilled or skilled manual workers.

Manufactured goods (commerce and finance)
The finished commercial products which have been manufactured from raw materials. They form an important part of Britain's industrial base and exports, although they have declined as a percentage of the total gross national product (GNP) since the late nineteenth century.

Marcopolo satellite (media)
See **Astra (satellite)**.

Marginal constituency (politics and government)
A parliamentary constituency, also referred to as a marginal seat, whose MP has been elected by a small majority (or margin) of the votes in a by-election or general election. Some constituencies have this status on a permanent basis, and the major parties concentrate their efforts here at election time.

Mark (education)
A grade (usually in percentage terms) which is given to a pupil or student as a result of an examination or test.

Market (commerce)
A collection of stalls, both indoors and in the open air, which sells a wide range of provisions and goods, and which is a feature of British life both in towns and the country.

Market and Opinion Research International (MORI) (society)
See **Public opinion polls**.

Market-maker (finance)
A member of the (London) Stock Exchange who buys and sells stocks and shares on the Stock Exchange, and also currencies on the currency exchanges. He or she generally deals with other traders from corporate offices in the City (of London). Market-makers will normally set a particular business trend or price in their dealings.

Market price (value) (finance and commerce)
The price which an object, service or product can fetch (or is valued at) on the open market when offered for sale.

Market Research Plan (Marplan) (society)
See **Public opinion polls**.

Market town (geography)
Usually a rural town that has historically held regular weekly markets, often in the open air on a central square or main street. The market comprises individual stalls which sell a wide variety of agricultural produce and manufactured goods.

Marks and Spencer (M and S) (commerce)
A well known store, founded in 1884, but now with branches throughout Britain which sell a wide range of their own quality clothing and food products. Known commonly as 'Marks and Sparks' or 'M and S'.

Marylebone Cricket Club, the (MCC) (sport and leisure)
One of Britain's oldest cricket clubs, founded in 1787. In later years

it was the most influential voice in world cricket and until 1969 was the governing body of cricket (now organized by the International Cricket Council [ICC]). It has its headquarters at Lord's cricket ground in London, which is also the home ground of Middlesex County Cricket Club.

Mass media (media)
A term to describe most forms of communications, but usually applied to the press (newspapers), radio and television.

Master (education)
1. The formal title (mistress if a female) of the head of a college, such as some of those which comprise Cambridge and Oxford Universities. 2. The title of a male schoolteacher (mistress if a female) in a school.

Master of Arts (MA) (education)
1. An intermediate higher degree granted by institutions of higher education in England and Wales to an individual who has usually studied a non-scientific subject. However, Oxford and Cambridge Universities award an MA to anyone who has an Oxford or Cambridge BA degree, on application after a period of time from graduation. 2. A first degree (the same as a BA elsewhere in Britain) awarded at some Scottish universities.

Master of foxhounds (MFH) (sport and leisure)
A person who supervises a pack of foxhounds (dogs) used in foxhunting, and who is normally responsible for the leadership and administration of a hunt in a local area.

Master of Science (MSc) (education)
An intermediate higher degree granted by many institutions of higher education to an individual who has studied a scientific or social science subject.

Master of the Queen's (King's) Music, the (royalty)
An honorary position held by a prominent musician who is appointed (normally by the sovereign after advice from the Prime Minister) to organize and compose music for the royal family on special occasions, such as coronations and royal weddings.

Master of the Rolls, the (MR) (law)
The senior civil law judge in England and Wales (appointed by the Crown on the advice of the Prime Minister) who is the head of the Court of Appeal (Civil Division), and ranks third after the Lord

Chancellor and the Lord Chief Justice in the legal hierarchy. He is the nominal official guardian of the national records at the Public Record Office, is a member of the Privy Council and formally admits solicitors to practise law (as Keeper of the Roll of Solicitors).

Maternity allowance (finance)
The state benefit (currently £42.45 a week) within the social security system which is paid for 18 weeks to a pregnant woman who is not eligible for maternity pay because she is unemployed or self-employed.

Maternity pay (employment and finance)
The statutory system whereby an employer is obliged at present to pay money for 6 weeks (at 90 per cent of salary) to a woman who takes leave from work to have a baby, and who has either been working full-time for the same employer for at least two years, or part-time for five years. A further 12 weeks is paid at a lower rate. Where a woman has been employed for between six months and two years she is entitled to payments for 18 weeks at the lower rate.

Matron (medicine)
The medically qualified person in charge of health care in a residential organization such as a boarding school, a rest home, nursing home or old people's home.

Mature student (education)
An adult student (usually over 20) who joins an institution of higher education several or many years after leaving school, or who studies on an adult or continuing education course.

May Day (society)
The first day of May in Britain is historically a rural occasion to celebrate the coming of spring, and has its roots in the country's agricultural and pagan past. Festivities may still be held in the countryside, at which a May Queen is elected. The first Monday following is a bank holiday (which may soon be abolished), on which political or industrial meetings and marches are held in towns and cities throughout Britain.

Mayor (government)
The leading municipal officer of a town, city or borough in England and Wales, who is usually elected on an honorary basis by councillors for one year. He or she (sometimes but infrequently known as a mayoress) may be the chairperson of the local council and per-

forms duties such as entertaining visitors, opening new buildings, schools and colleges, and attending church services or ceremonial occasions as the local representative. In a number of large English cities the mayor is called the lord mayor. In Scotland the duties of a mayor are performed by a provost or in some large cities those of a lord mayor by a lord provost.

Maze Prison, the (law)
See **H-blocks.**

Means test (finance)
A system whereby an applicant for a grant of money has other income taken into account in order to arrive at an appropriate sum for the grant, such as an applicant for legal aid, a student applying for a student grant where the parents' income is relevant, or an applicant for income support.

Medical Research Council, the (MRC) (medicine)
The body, set up in 1920, which operates under a royal charter and carries out biomedical research in its own research institutes. It also establishes and finances research units in medical schools, hospitals and higher education institutions.

Member of Parliament (MP) (government)
A member of the House of Commons (not the House of Lords) who has been elected by the voters in a parliamentary constituency to be their representative. In addition to supporting his or her political party in Parliament, a constituency MP is also supposed to look after the interests of all the constituents whether they voted for him or her or not.

Member of the European Parliament (MEP) (government)
See **Euro-MP.**

Merchant bank (finance)
A specialist and frequently long-established bank, which provides financial and commercial advice and aid to business, both in Britain and overseas, in areas such as international trade, takeovers, mergers and share flotations on the (London) Stock Exchange.

Mercury (Communications Ltd) (communications)
A private telecommunications system which was specially established in 1983 to compete with British Telecom (BT) following the latter's privatization, and which provides similar services, such as telephones and data communications.

Merger (commerce)
See **Monopolies and Mergers Commission**.

Methodist Church, the (religion)
The Church was established in 1729 by the evangelical preacher John Wesley as a reaction against the restraints and formalism of the Church of England. The present Church is the largest of the Free Churches and is based on the 1932 amalgamation of most of the then separate Methodist Churches. It has some 450,000 adult full members, who are known as Methodists.

Metropolitan district councils (government)
Local government areas in England which are subdivisions of the old metropolitan county councils abolished in 1986 (but which remain as identifiable territorial units), and which now largely perform the work of those former councils. Six conurbations were named as metropolitan counties in the 1974 reorganization of local government: Merseyside (centred on Liverpool), Greater Manchester, West Midlands (centred on Birmingham), West Yorkshire (centred on Leeds and Bradford), South Yorkshire (centred on Sheffield) and Tyne and Wear (centred on Newcastle).

Metropolitan Police, the (Met) (law)
The police force (commonly known as the Met) which is in charge of policing London (except for the City of London which has its own independent force), with its headquarters at New Scotland Yard. It is Britain's oldest force founded in 1829 by the then Home Secretary Sir Robert Peel. The earliest policemen in London were nicknamed peelers, and later bobbies after Peel, and today the Met is still the responsibility of the Home Secretary although its operational head is the Commissioner of Police.

MI5/MI6 (government)
The commonly used names (standing for Military Intelligence, sections 5 and 6) of the counter-intelligence (or secret) service of the British government, which has now been brought more closely under parliamentary control. MI5 deals with domestic security matters within Britain (including Northern Ireland), and MI6 gathers intelligence in other countries.

Middle class (society)
A widely based and expanding social class in Britain which is generally considered by researchers and the public to be above working class and below upper class, and sometimes split into upper and

lower middle class. It includes a range of businessmen, clerical workers and professional people, although more occupational groups are now being regarded as middle class.

Middle school (education)
Some local educational authorities divide their state comprehensive system into middle schools for pupils aged between 9 and 12/14 after which they transfer to a senior comprehensive school.

Midland (Bank), the (finance)
One of the five leading English banks, founded in 1836, with branches in towns and cities throughout Britain, providing financial services for private and commercial customers.

Midwife (medicine)
A professionally qualified person employed by the NHS or local health authority who provides services, help and advice for women during the child-bearing period (ante- and post-natal), in hospitals, clinics and the home.

Militant Tendency, the (politics)
A Trotskyite or extreme left-wing political party, which has infiltrated the Labour Party over the years but whose members have now been progressively expelled from Labour.

Military Tattoo (Edinburgh), the (military, sport and leisure)
See **Edinburgh**.

Milkman/woman (society)
An important daily institution in British life. A man or woman who delivers fresh milk and other dairy products early every day in most regions of Britain to private houses and business premises, usually by means of a small vehicle called a milk-float.

Mini-budget (government)
A brief government budget or financial statement which occurs usually in the autumn midway between two annual budgets. It often contains amendments and corrections to the government's economic plans.

Minister (religion and government)
1. An ordained clergyman in the Free Churches. 2. Many members of the government are formally appointed as ministers of the Crown. The term can refer both to a government minister who heads a government ministry and to a secretary of state (or senior minister) who heads a government department. The latter will have

ministers under him or her to help with the running of the department. A member of the government, such as the Chancellor of the Duchy of Lancaster, who does not have many ministerial or departmental responsibilities, is also a minister of the Crown.

Ministerial responsibility (government)
This parliamentary convention is divided into two. Individual ministerial responsibility is where the minister in charge of a department or ministry is personally responsible to Parliament for the workings of that department or ministry. Collective responsibility is that owed by all ministers, including those in the Cabinet, for the policies and actions of the sitting government.

Ministry (government)
1. A government department or ministry headed by a minister or a secretary of state. Most former ministries are now called departments. 2. The actual building where such a department is centred, usually in Whitehall or central London.

Ministry of Transport Test, the (MOT) (transport)
The still commonly used term for the annual test of all private motor vehicles which are over 3 years old (5 years in Northern Ireland) to ensure that they are safe and in good working condition. They must be tested at authorized private garages (or at official inspection centres in Northern Ireland). Heavy goods vehicles (HGVs) must also undergo annual specialist tests. The testing of vehicles to determine their roadworthiness is the job of the Vehicle Inspectorate under the Secretary of State for Transport.

Minor (law)
A young person (known also as an infant) under the age of 18, who is legally incapable of certain functions, such as voting, owning property or making a will.

Minority government (government)
The situation which arises in Britain when a political party (such as Labour or the Conservatives) has achieved a small (although not overall) majority of parliamentary seats in the House of Commons over other parties in a general election, and can manage to form a (minority) government. It is then usually dependent upon the votes of smaller parties (such as the Liberal Democrats and Nationalist parties) to remain in power.

Minster (religion)
A distinctive term used to describe some Church of England

cathedrals (such as York Minster) and large Anglican churches which were historically attached to, or part of, a monastery (such as Beverley Minster on Humberside).

Mitigation (law)
At the end of a criminal trial in which the accused person has been found guilty of an offence, the defence lawyer may attempt to reduce the eventual sentence of the court by offering a speech in mitigation. This will present personal information and other reasons to explain why, for example, the accused should be fined instead of being sent to prison, or suffer no penalty at all.

Mixed economy (commerce)
The term used to describe the British economy which is divided (mixed) into the public (state) sector and the private sector. Over two-thirds of the economy is now in the private sector and under one-third in the public.

Mode of trial enquiry (law)
The process whereby the magistrates in a magistrates' court in England and Wales decide whether they have the powers to judge a case themselves or whether the matter must be sent to the crown court because of its seriousness and their limited sentencing powers. In certain either-or cases the accused can elect to be tried before the crown court instead of the magistrates' court.

Moderator of the Church of Scotland (religion)
The leader and spokesperson of the Church of Scotland who is elected for one year, and who leads the General Assembly (annual meeting) of the Church.

Monarch (royalty)
An alternative term for a sovereign, which can be applied both to a king and a queen.

Monopolies and Mergers Commission, the (government and commerce)
A statutory organization, established in 1948, with independent members appointed by the government which examines the effects of monopolies and mergers on the public interest. It investigates (if asked), and prepares reports on, any potentially unlawful or undesirable monopoly or merger which curtails free trading conditions and competition in both the private and state sectors of the national economy. A monopoly is the dominant control of products and services by a small number of people, while a merger between

groups results in the common ownership of several companies. The commission has power to reject a proposed merger or monopoly situation.

Monthlies, the (media)
A term to describe magazines and journals which appear once a month, such as *Vogue* or *Which?*.

Mortgage (finance)
A legal agreement for a financial loan from a building society or other lending institution which enables the borrower to buy a house or flat and obtain tax relief on the loan up to £30,000. He or she must repay the loan in monthly instalments (including both capital and interest). An inability to do so means that the lender can legally obtain ownership of (repossess) the house.

Motor Show, the (transport)
An international exhibition where the latest cars and motoring equipment (British and foreign) are on display. It takes place every two years at the National Exhibition Centre (NEC), Birmingham, an important exhibition and conference centre established in 1976.

Motorway (transport)
A major road, with multiple traffic lanes in both directions and extensive service and rest facilities, which carries cars and heavy vehicles, and provides a road connection between large cities. Access to motorways from external roads is made by special linking roads (slip roads), and pedestrians, L-drivers or cyclists are banned from using them. Motorways are individually numbered, such as the M1 (London to the north of England) and the M4 (London to South Wales).

Multinational (commerce)
A company operating in Britain which has international branches in many countries abroad, and which may have its registered head-quarters outside Britain.

Murrayfield (sport and leisure)
The sports ground and stadium of the Scottish Rugby Union in Edinburgh, regarded as the national centre for the Scottish game.

N

National Bus Company, the (NBC) (transport)
A private bus and coach company in England and Wales created when the former state service was privatized in 1987–8. It is divided into some 70 regional branches and has a profitable national network of long-distance coach services.

National Car Parks (NCP) (commerce and transport)
A private commercial company that provides paying car park facilities (usually in multi-level buildings in town and city centres) throughout Britain.

National Consumer Council, the (NCC) (commerce)
A government-financed, but independent and non-statutory body in England, established in 1975, which monitors consumer matters and represents the consumer's view to government and industry. It co-operates with similar councils in Scotland, Wales and Northern Ireland.

National Curriculum, the (education)
The centralized study programme which is gradually being introduced at primary and secondary levels in all state schools in England and Wales under the Education Reform Act 1988, in a governmental attempt to improve educational standards. It has the core subjects of English, mathematics and science as its base, and also covers the additional seven foundation subjects of history, geography, technology, music, art, physical education and (at secondary school level) a modern foreign language. Attainment targets are being set for each subject, with tests for pupils at the ages of 7, 11, 14 and 16. The National Curriculum is also closely tied to national examinations such as the GCSE. Similar common curriculum systems are also being introduced in Scotland and Northern Ireland, and are being followed in the independent school sector.

National Debt, the (finance and government)
Historically this means an accumulated state debt beginning in 1693 which has not been paid off. Today governments borrow money from the public to finance government spending which cannot be covered by state revenue. The shortfall between the two (income

and spending) is known as the public sector borrowing requirement (PSBR), and the necessary loans are raised by the sale of government certificates and gilt-edged securities.

National Exhibition Centre, the (NEC) (commerce)
See **Motor Show**.

National Farmers' Union, the (NFU) (employment)
An organization with a current membership of some 120,000, founded in 1908 to support and campaign for the interests of its farmer-members in England and Wales, but which is not a trade union. Scotland has an independent NFU.

National Front, the (NF) (politics)
A small, extreme right-wing political party established in 1966, which draws its support mainly from the disaffected, unemployed and underprivileged sections of British society. It sees itself as a patriotic nationalist party, and campaigns for the expulsion of coloured immigrants from Britain, argues against further immigration, wants the establishment of strong law-and-order policies and is against the European Community. Its critics see it as violent, xenophobic and racist, and it has no representation in Parliament.

National Gallery, the (NG) (London and arts)
A large and well known government-subsidized art gallery in Trafalgar Square, London. It was established in 1824 and contains extensive collections of British and foreign art, with the biggest number of paintings in Britain.

National Girobank, the (finance)
A banking and money transfer organization formerly operated by the Post Office, but now a private subsidiary of the Alliance and Leicester Building Society, with credit transfer and other services for private and business customers. It was originally established in 1968 and functions through post offices and banks.

National Health Service, the (NHS) (medicine)
The nationwide system of free state primary medical services established in 1948. It is largely financed by taxation and national insurance (NI), and allows people to obtain medical treatment from doctors and in hospitals. However, charges may be made for prescriptions, eye tests and dental care in some cases.

National insurance (NI) (finance)
The national system of compulsory financial contributions mainly

by employees and employers (but also the self-employed in some cases) out of which state sickness, retirement, unemployment and other benefits are provided. Individuals pay a percentage of their gross income to the scheme.

National parks (geography)
The 10 areas of countryside amounting to some 9 per cent of the land in England and Wales where the countryside is conserved and protected under legislation, but to which the public has access and where recreational facilities are provided. Most of the parks cover scenic regions of hill or mountain country, moorland or forest, such as Snowdonia in northern Wales, the Lake District in north-west England, and Dartmoor in south-west England.

National Portrait Gallery, the (NPG) (London and arts)
An art gallery in London, opened in 1859, which contains extensive collections of portraits (original paintings and photographs) of distinguished individuals in British history.

National Power (science and commerce)
See **Electricity supplies**.

National Savings Bank, the (NSB) (finance)
A state savings bank organized by the Post Office which provides many investment options at its local post offices throughout Britain, like National Savings Certificates and Premium Bonds.

National Savings Certificates (finance)
Investment certificates from the National Savings Bank which are sold to individuals at post offices throughout Britain, and which are held for a specific number of years. They are attractive to small investors because they give either a fixed or increasing rate of interest over the period on which no income tax is payable.

National scenic area (geography)
The 40 areas of countryside in Scotland covering some 13 per cent of the country that are the counterparts of the national parks in England and Wales, and in which only limited development is permitted.

National Theatre, the (NT) (arts)
A state-subsidized theatre company, which since 1976 has performed classical and modern plays in its own building (consisting of three auditoriums) on the South Bank, London. It produces the most plays of any theatre company in the country.

National Trust, the (NT) (society)
An independent voluntary organization (the National Trust for
Places of Historic Interest or Natural Beauty), with a current membership of some 1.5 million, established in 1895 to preserve historic
buildings and monuments as well as rural areas in England, Wales
and Northern Ireland. It acquires and maintains property (such as
country houses), land and coastal areas, canals and gardens, which
are open to the public. The National Trust for Scotland (NTS),
founded in 1931, does a similar job in Scotland.

National Union of Students, the (NUS) (education)
An independent association for students with over 1 million members in further and higher education, which was established in 1922
and functions through local branches in educational institutions
throughout Britain. It serves the general social and educational
interests of students, and membership fees are deducted from the
student grant.

National Westminster Bank, the (NatWest) (finance)
One of the five leading English banks, established in its present
form in 1968, with branches in towns and cities throughout Britain
which provide banking services for individual and commercial customers.

National Youth Orchestra, the (NYO) (the arts)
The NYO comprises the National Youth Orchestras of Great Britain, Scotland and Wales. These bodies provide young professional
musicians with orchestral experience and have achieved high standards. They co-operate with, and are organized through, a system
of local and regional youth orchestras throughout the country.

National Youth Theatre, the (NYT) (the arts)
There are several hundred youth theatres throughout Britain, which
operate collectively under the NYT, a leading company that provides young professional actors with stage experience at the Shaw
Theatre in north-west London. The Scottish Youth Theatre in Glasgow performs a similar role.

Nationalist parties (politics)
Those political parties such as the Scottish National Party (SNP)
and Plaid Cymru in Wales which campaign for parliamentary seats
only in their own countries and have specific nationalist interests
and manifestos, such as devolution and/or independence for Wales
and Scotland.

Nationalized industries, the (commerce and government)
Britain's current nationalized industries are mainly those established
by Labour governments after 1945 under their policy of nationalization (transferring private companies to public or state ownership,
now sometimes called social ownership). Conservative governments
have also nationalized certain industries, so that the present state-
run concerns are those like the Bank of England (BE), British Rail
(BR), British Coal (BC), British Shipbuilders and the Post Office
(PO). But the Conservative government from 1979 has promoted
a policy of privatization, or selling off state-owned industries to
private ownership, such as the former nationalized industries British
Aerospace (BAe), British Gas, British Petroleum (BP), British
Steel (BS), the British Airports Authority (BAA), British Telecom
(BT), British Airways (BA) and the electricity and water supplies.

Natural History Museum, the (London)
Britain's major natural history museum in London which was established at its present location in 1881. It contains extensive collections of zoological, botanical, mineral and other natural history
artefacts (such as dinosaur reconstructions), and organizes educational programmes, exhibitions and lectures.

Naturalization (law and society)
The legal process whereby a citizen of a foreign country is formally
and legally able to acquire British nationality, normally after a
period of residence, and having a knowledge of English and no
criminal convictions.

Nature Conservancy Council, the (geography)
See **Nature reserves**.

Nature reserves (geography)
Some 240 areas of particular botanical or zoological interest and
importance in Britain, where the conservation of rare plant and
animal life is prioritized and co-ordinated by a statutory body (the
Nature Conservancy Council), originally established in 1949.

Neighbourhood Watch (society)
A voluntary association of local residents in areas throughout Britain whose members watch over houses and property in the local
neighbourhood. The intention is to reduce or prevent crime and to
help the police by reporting suspicious behaviour.

New Commonwealth, the (politics)
A collective term used to describe those Commonwealth countries,

such as India, Pakistan and the nations of the West Indies, which achieved their independence from British colonial rule later than Old Commonwealth nations, such as Australia, Canada and New Zealand.

New Scotland Yard (law)
The headquarters since 1966 of the London Metropolitan Police Force in Westminster, London, which contains the central departments of the force, and from where most of the policing of the capital is co-ordinated.

New Towns (geography and housing)
The term associated with those specially designed and planned towns constructed in Britain since 1900 (which were known as garden cities in the early stages of this development) and particularly since 1946 by successive British governments. The intention was to create living and business opportunities for industry and people in a rural environment outside the congested and decaying large cities. Some 32 New Towns have been built since 1946.

New Year's Eve (society)
A traditional time (31 December) for celebrations throughout Britain (Hogmanay in Scotland) to welcome in the New Year, but which is not a bank holiday. The festivities may be held in private or in public, such as those in Trafalgar Square (a large public square in central London with a statue of the sea hero Lord Nelson commemorating his victory over the French at the Battle of Trafalgar in 1805).

Newmarket (sport and leisure)
The town in Suffolk that has traditionally been identified with British horse-racing. It has a well known racecourse, the headquarters of the Jockey Club, the National Horse-racing Museum, horse sales and auction facilities, and the stables of leading trainers and horse owners.

Newsagent (commerce and media)
See **Paperboy/papergirl**.

Nirex (science and commerce)
See **Nuclear power**.

Nonconformists (religion)
Historically those members of Protestant Churches who refused to conform to the practices and belief of the established national

Church (that is, the Church of England) such as the Methodists, the Baptists and the United Reformed Church. They dissented and formed their own Churches, better known today as the Free Churches.

North Atlantic Treaty Organization, the (NATO) (military)
British defence policy has been founded on that of NATO since the organization was formed in 1952. NATO is a defensive alliance of 16 western nations which will respond to aggression in self-defence if one of its members is attacked. The future of NATO is uncertain, but it has already been converted into a leaner, flexible-response organization, and it may become more a political grouping than a military one.

North Sea gas (science)
Natural gas extracted via pipe lines from gas fields under the North Sea off the east coasts of England and Scotland by independent multinational companies under licence from the British government. Supplies of natural gas have now wholly replaced the gas that was formerly manufactured from coal in Britain.

North Sea oil (science)
Crude oil extracted via pipe lines from oil fields beneath the North Sea off the east coasts of England and Scotland by independent multinational companies under licence from the British government. Britain was formerly dependent upon oil imports, but from the mid-1970s has become self-sufficient domestically and an oil exporter.

Northern Ireland (NI) (geography and government)
Before 1921 Northern Ireland (current population 1,570,000) was part of the whole island of Ireland, and was historically the ancient Kingdom of Ulster. After English and Scottish colonization from the sixteenth century, Northern Ireland became predominantly Protestant, while the rest of Ireland remained mainly Roman Catholic. By the Anglo-Irish treaty of 1921 Ireland was partitioned and Northern Ireland remained part of the United Kingdom with its own Protestant-dominated Parliament. But since 1972 it has been governed directly by the British government in London.

Northern Ireland Assembly, the (government)
The body (1982–6), elected by proportional representation, that was intended to restore self-government (based on power-sharing between Protestants and Catholics) to Northern Ireland following the imposition of direct rule by the British government in 1972.

But neither Protestant nor Catholic members for various reasons were prepared to support the assembly. It was dissolved by the British government in 1986 and direct rule from Westminster continued. However, talks on possible power-sharing are continuing, and a new assembly (or equivalent body) might be formed.

North–South divide, the (geography and society)
The term which has been recently used to describe the alleged social, economic and political differences between the north and the south of England. The north is supposed to have higher unemployment, a bigger crime rate, lower standards of living, cheaper houses and to vote Labour. The south is credited with less unemployment, less crime, higher standards of living, more expensive houses and voting Conservative.

Not proven (law)
The verdict delivered by a Scottish jury in a criminal case, which is an addition to the decisions of guilty and not guilty, when the evidence in the case is insufficient to prove or disprove the charge against an accused person.

Notting Hill Carnival, the (society)
A large annual West Indian festival of street music, parades and parties which has taken place in Notting Hill, West London, on the August Bank Holiday weekend since 1966. It is a generally peaceful event, although there have been periodic clashes with the police.

Nuclear power (science)
Britain has had a domestic nuclear power programme since 1956 when its first nuclear power station at Calder Hall in north-west England started supplying electricity nationwide. There are currently some 16 nuclear power stations controlled by the publicly owned Nuclear Electric plc nuclear generator in England and Wales and Scottish Nuclear in Scotland, consisting of old- and new-style stations. In 1992 plans for the further expansion of nuclear facilities were postponed to the mid-1990s. The Nuclear Industry Radioactive Waste Disposal Executive (Nirex) is in charge of nuclear waste disposal.

Nursery school (education)
A school (sometimes known as a kindergarten) for young children (3–5 years old) which some are able to attend before compulsory state education starts at the age of 5. Such schools may be private

or run by the local authority, but the state provides for only some 45 per cent of children in the age group on a nationwide basis.

Nurses (medicine)

After a minimum training of three years a student in Britain qualifies as a registered general nurse, and is able to work in the general health services. Specialization in other branches of medicine, such as midwifery and some aspects of surgery, requires extra training and qualifications. The Royal College of Nursing (RCN) is the nurses' main trade union or professional association.

O

Offer (science and commerce)
See **Electricity supplies**.

Office of Fair Trading, the (OFT) (government)
The government agency under a Director of Fair Trading, established in 1973, that monitors trading practices, commercial activities, advertising, and the supply of goods and services in Britain. It can and does recommend government action in these areas, is an influential body which protects the rights of consumers, and has contributed to higher standards in commercial life.

Official Secrets Act, the (law)
The law, continuously updated since 1911 with the latest Act in 1989, which prohibits harmful actions against the security interests of the state, such as the publishing or communicating of secret information. If found guilty of such a criminal offence, the person/ organization may be imprisoned and/or fined. Individuals employed in sensitive government establishments and in security-based jobs are obliged to sign and obey the Official Secrets Act.

Official strike (employment)
A strike called by the executive of a trade union which has been approved (and therefore legalized) by a secret written ballot of all its members.

Off-licence (commerce)
A shop or store licensed by local magistrates to sell alcoholic drinks to people aged 18 and over for consumption off the premises.

Ofgas (science and commerce)
See **British Gas plc**.

Oftel (communications)
See **British Telecom**.

Ofwat (science and commerce)
See **Water supplies**.

Old age pension, the (finance)
The state pension which is paid to all employed men on retirement

at 65 and to all employed women at 60. The money is raised from the compulsory national insurance contributions paid during the person's working life. A woman who has not held a job can receive a pension herself but usually a married couple will receive a joint pension. Discussions are continuing on how best to equalize the retirement age for both sexes.

Old age pensioner (OAP) (society)
A retired man or woman aged 65 and over or 60 and over respectively (often known as a senior citizen or OAP) who receives the state pension. Pensioners receive certain services at reduced rates such as rail travel, cheaper admission fees to cinemas or exhibitions, and some free goods or services, such as bus travel and medical services. An additional payment, known as a Christmas bonus (currently £10), is also made before Christmas to all OAPs.

Old Bailey, the (law)
See **Central Criminal Court**.

Old boy/girl (education)
A former pupil of a secondary school, whether state or independent. He or she may remain in contact with the school, receive news and attend functions by joining a voluntary organization of former students.

Old boy network (society)
Former pupils/students of a particular school or university bound together by the group identity of that institution. The network of contacts and influence of such a group may be used to gain advantages which are not available to outsiders. Today the term may also include females.

Old Commonwealth, the (politics)
The name given to those large former colonies of the British Empire, such as Canada, Australia and New Zealand, which have predominantly white populations and which achieved their independence from Britain earlier than other colonies (such as those of the New Commonwealth).

Old people's homes (society)
Residential homes and nursing homes (with health and medical facilities) for elderly people. Such homes are provided in both the public and the private sectors by local government or commercial companies.

Old school tie (education)
A tie worn by an old boy which identifies him as a former pupil at a school. It is supposed to represent loyalty to, and the values of, the school. The term is not generally associated with old girls.

Ombudsman, the (government)
The common name of the Parliamentary Commissioner for Administration (PCA), a government-appointed independent official who investigates complaints from members of the public who allege that they have been ill-treated by a central government department. The ombudsman system has now spread to include insurance companies, local government, health services (the NHS), solicitors, children and banks.

One-parent family (society)
A family with one or more children in which there is only one adult (male or female) to look after them. Some 90 per cent of these families have a woman as the head.

Open College, the (education)
A government-sponsored educational institution with programmes on television and radio at relatively basic levels which began in 1987. It is designed to help people over 16 on the employment market by providing further education, courses in reading and maths, and special vocational training. The students follow correspondence courses connected to the broadcast series.

Open day (society and education)
An occasion when the general public may visit a closed institution such as a school, factory, university, local council offices or military base, and when events are provided to illustrate the working of the institution.

Open University, the (OU) (education)
A non-residential university established by the Labour government in 1969 in Milton Keynes, Buckinghamshire. It gives an opportunity to all those who wish to study on a part-time basis for a degree, and students are not required to have the formal qualifications for entry to higher education. Students pursue their degree studies through correspondence courses linked to radio and television programmes, and by meetings with and the submission of written work to local tutors. They may also have to attend short intensive summer schools.

Opening (State), the (of Parliament) (government)
The official state ceremony when a new session of Parliament
(usually annually in the autumn or after a general election) is
formally opened by the monarch. The sovereign travels in procession to the Houses of Parliament for the occasion, and makes
the Speech from the Throne (outlining the government's legislative
programme for the coming session) in the House of Lords to the
combined Lords and Commons.

Opposition, (Official) the (government)
The second largest political party in the House of Commons after
the government (usually either the Conservatives or the Labour
Party) forms the official opposition to the sitting government, and
its spokesmen/women sit directly opposite the government benches.
It has an elected Official Leader of the Opposition and a Shadow
Cabinet, and is formally known as Her Majesty's Loyal Opposition.

Opposition parties, the (politics)
All those political parties in Parliament which do not form the
sitting government and which sit on the opposition benches in the
Houses of Commons and Lords. Currently these consist of the
Labour Party, the Liberal Democrats, the Scottish and Welsh
Nationalists, and the Northern Irish parties.

Opting out (government)
A policy introduced by the Conservative government in the 1980s
whereby institutions, although continuing to be state organizations,
are allowed to transfer from local authority control and become
self-governing with their own budgets granted directly from central
government (grant-maintained status). This has happened in education where some state schools, and in health where some NHS
hospitals, have opted out of local government or local health
authority control.

Oracle (media)
See **Teletext**.

Orangemen (politics)
Members of the Orange Society (or Order), a political association
of Protestants in Northern Ireland (and elsewhere in Britain and
overseas) whose aim is to maintain Protestantism. The society
was established in 1795, and was named after the Dutch Protestant
King William III (William of Orange) who defeated the Catholic
forces of James II at the Battle of the Boyne in 1690. The society

commemorates the battle with an annual parade in Northern Ireland on 12 July.

Order in council (government)
A declaration made formally by the sovereign in the Privy Council, which in most cases is a decision of the Cabinet or government made formally through the Privy Council. Orders may cover a wide range of government and state business.

Order paper (government)
A printed document which gives the order in which daily parliamentary business, debates and votes are to be arranged and decided in the House of Commons, and which is circulated to all MPs.

Ordinary shares (finance)
Shares issued by a company (whether public or private) which are bought and which give their holders a right to a part (or dividend) of the company's declared profits. This is made after the payment of a dividend to preference and other special shareholders, whom the company is obliged to compensate first.

Ordnance Survey, the (OS) (geography)
A government organization, founded in 1791, which produces maps for official and public bodies, and the general public. It originally published its well known 'inch to a mile' maps of Britain in the mid-nineteenth century during the Napoleonic Wars, which have now been replaced by the larger-scale metric '2 cm to 1 km' maps.

Outward Bound Trust, the (education)
A voluntary body established in 1946 by Kurt Hahn (who also founded the Scottish public school Gordonstoun) that organizes outdoor physical activities for young people, such as sailing, canoeing, rock climbing and orienteering, with the aim of developing individual initiative and sense of teamwork.

Oval, the (sport and leisure)
A famous cricket ground at Kennington, South London, first used in 1845, and now the headquarters of the Surrey County Cricket Club where county and test matches are played.

Overall majority (government and politics)
See **Majority**.

Oxbridge (education)
A common name for the two universities of Cambridge and Oxford, used to indicate their special ethos, standards and traditions.

Oxford English Dictionary, the (OED) (language)
Traditionally the most authoritative and comprehensive standard dictionary of the English language, published by the Oxford University Press, part by part from 1884 onwards, and completed in 1928. New and additional volumes have appeared since, with a new second edition in 1989, together with smaller, abridged, special and adapted versions.

Oxford Movement, the (religion)
A religious movement begun in Oxford by Anglican theologians and clergy in 1833, which emphasized the historical connection and doctrinal origins of the Church of England with the Roman Catholic Church, and which was associated with High Church beliefs and practice.

Oxford University (OU) (education)
One of the two oldest and best known universities (with Cambridge University) in England. It has a collegiate structure with some 35 colleges, like Christ Church, Magdalen and Balliol, the earliest of which were established in the twelfth century. Two are for women only, and the rest are coeducational. There are currently some 10,000 students attending the university, of whom nearly half are women.

Owner-occupier (housing)
A person who owns the house or property in which he or she lives, as opposed to renting it from another owner.

P

Pairing (government)
The arrangement by which a member of one political party in the House of Commons agrees with a member of another party that their votes will match each other's, so that both need not be in the chamber of the House all the time to record their individual votes. This system is mainly applicable to Labour and Conservative MPs.

Palladium (London), the (arts)
A well known London theatre, which presents international and domestic theatrical shows that are often televised and patronized by the royal family. It is synonymous with British light entertainment, and the music hall and variety theatre tradition.

Panel (medicine)
The number of NHS patients for which a general practitioner (GP) is responsible, normally about 2,000, and on which his or her salary is calculated.

Pantomime (society and arts)
A musical play or dramatic entertainment within a traditional fairy-tale story-line such as *Jack and the Beanstalk* or *Cinderella*, which is performed annually in the Christmas holiday season in theatres and other venues by professionals and amateurs, and is very popular with children. The current pantomime tradition, in which male and female roles are reversed for some parts, is about a century old.

Paperboy/papergirl (society and media)
A boy or girl who is paid by a newsagent (newspaper shop owner) to deliver newspapers and magazines daily in the early morning and late afternoon to private houses and offices. Customers order the papers through and pay the cost (including usually an added delivery charge) to the newsagent, normally on a weekly basis.

Papworth Hospital (medicine)
See **Harefield Hospital**.

Parent-teacher association (PTA) (education)
A body established by many schools which allows parents of school-

children and their teachers to meet regularly to discuss the children's progress and school policy.

Parish (government and religion)
The smallest unit of local government in England (and formerly Wales), which is a subdivision of a district or county. It was historically centred on a village church after England's conversion to Christianity in the sixth century. Today rural parishes which have elected parish councils have some local government responsibility, but the urban parishes generally have none, existing only as church units.

Parish church (religion)
The particular church belonging to a parish unit which is attended by churchgoers living in that area. Rural villages may have only one parish church (normally of the Church of England in England), while parishes in the larger towns and cities have several, each belonging to a different denomination.

Parish magazine (religion)
A regular publication, usually written and distributed by a parish priest and members of the parish church, which provides information for parish members, such as church services and announcements of births, marriages and deaths.

Parish register (religion)
A set of books (often going back centuries and kept at a parish church) in which the baptisms, marriages and burials in the parish are traditionally documented.

Parliament (government)
The supreme law-making body of the British governmental system (except for some law deriving from superior European Community institutions) comprising the House of Commons, the House of Lords and (formally) the monarch. Parliament also scrutinizes the workings and policies of the sitting government, and controls public revenue.

Parliamentary Commissioner for Administration, the (PCA)
(government)
See **Ombudsman**.

Parliamentary private secretary (PPS) (government)
A Member of Parliament (MP) and backbencher (usually a junior member of the House of Commons) who is chosen by a minister

to act as the latter's secretary and adviser. This is normally the first step in an MP's rise to ministerial office.

Parliamentary secretary (government)
A Member of Parliament (MP) who serves as a junior minister and deputy for a senior minister who is not a secretary of state, and who has official responsibilities in the ministry or department. This is usually the first governmental post for many future heads of departments and ministries. The MP is known as a parliamentary under-secretary of state when his or her senior minister is a secretary of state.

Parochial church council (PCC) (religion)
The administrative or governing body of a parish church in the Church of England, comprising elected members of the church.

Parson (religion)
A term commonly used for ordained clergymen or priests in the Church of England.

Partnership (commerce)
A business relationship between at least two people who run a business for profit. They own the business and are responsible for its profits and losses, in distinction to a company which is owned by its shareholders.

Patent Office, the (PO) (government)
The ancient office (now a government agency) which controls the issuing of patents (legal rights over new inventions) to commercial companies and individual inventors.

Patrol car (law)
The name for a car which a police force uses for patrolling a local police district or region. It may also be called a panda car because of its colour and stripings.

Pay As You Earn (PAYE) (finance)
Part of the state income tax system when the amount of an individual employee's liability to income tax is deducted at source from his or her pay or wage by the employer, who then forwards the deducted money to the Inland Revenue (IR).

Pay beds (medicine)
The arrangement whereby patients can pay for their medical treatment in a state NHS hospital and have private facilities. This was

a concession to doctors who wished to retain some private patients when the NHS was established in 1946–7.

Paymaster-General, the (government)
The minister who heads the government accounting office (the Paymaster-General's Office) which oversees the financial and banking transactions carried out by government departments (except for the Inland Revenue and Customs and Excise), and which acts as the paying agent for all government departments.

Peer (society and government)
1. Hereditary peer: those members of the aristocracy who at the age of 21 have an automatic right to take their seats and to speak and vote in the House of Lords. On a peer's death the title normally passes to the male relation next in the line of succession, like the eldest son. However, a woman can inherit a title in her own right and is called a lady peer or peeress. Since 1963 hereditary peers may renounce their titles during their lifetime, but the title continues and can be inherited in the future. 2. Life peers: a) those members of the House of Lords, with the right to speak and vote, who have been created peers for their lifetimes normally on the recommendation of a political party. b) Those peers in the House of Lords who hold special office, such as the two archbishops and 24 senior bishops of the Church of England (the Lords Spiritual), and the Law Lords.

Peerage (society)
The various ranks of peers in England, Scotland, Ireland, Great Britain (since 1707) and the United Kingdom (since 1801), both hereditary and life, with titles such as duke, marquess, earl, viscount and baron (or baroness), and who may sit in the House of Lords. Irish peers who do not possess an additional non-Irish rank, cannot now sit in the House.

Penal system, the (law)
Britain's criminal punishment system comprises the custodial (imprisonment) and the non-custodial (without imprisonment). Non-custodial sentences from a court are mostly fines (monetary punishment), probation, community service and absolute discharge (freedom with no conditions). Custodial sentences from a court mean imprisonment for a variable period of time up to life (or 21 years). Prisoners with medium-term sentences may be released on parole, and prisoners serving life sentences may be released on licence, in both cases after serving part of their sentences. Famous

prisons are Pentonville for men and Holloway for women in London, Parkhurst on the Isle of Wight for long-term prisoners, and Dartmoor. Britain currently has the highest prison population in western Europe.

Penalty points (law and transport)
A government legal system which punishes bad driving on Britain's roads, and is largely operated by the magistrates' courts. Driving offences, such as speeding, are given a specific number of penalty points which are entered on the driver's licence. When the accumulated points reach a certain total the driver is automatically disqualified from driving for a period of time.

Penguin paperback (arts and commerce)
Penguin Books (established in 1935) was the first company in Britain to publish serious fiction and quality books in paper covers at a relatively low price. The concept of paperback publishing (in contrast to hardback) has since spread, but prices have also increased considerably.

Permanent secretary (government)
The rank of the chief civil servant in government departments, and the senior post in the administrative grade of the Civil Service. Such an appointment must be approved by the Prime Minister, and is a very influential position.

Personal column (media)
A section of a newspaper or magazine, usually in the advertising pages, where individuals may have personal announcements or messages inserted for a fee.

Personal pension plan (PPP) (finance)
An arrangement whereby a person who is not a member of an occupational (or company) pension scheme is able to make personal pension arrangements up to specified levels, in addition to his or her state pension.

Pickets (employment)
A small number of workers or trade unionists who are posted outside their place of work during a strike or other industrial dispute. In law their numbers must now be restricted and they can only attempt to dissuade other employees, clients or suppliers from entering the premises.

Pinewood Studios, the (arts)
An extensive area of film studios, sets and locations in Buckingham-

shire, established in 1936. It has traditionally been the centre of the British film industry, but has declined in importance in recent years.

Plaid Cymru (politics)
The main Welsh nationalist party (meaning 'the party of Wales') established in 1925 which fights for the political separation of Wales from the United Kingdom and for Welsh self-government through its own legislature. Its aim is to preserve and safeguard the Welsh language, culture, traditions, economic resources and national identity. Currently it has four MPs in the House of Commons.

Plaintiff (law)
The person in a civil law action who initiates a claim against a defendant, usually for a specific sum of money in damages.

Planning permission (law)
The authority given by a local government council at county or district level to an individual or company wishing to make substantial changes to property, or to construct buildings and other permanent structures.

Playground (education)
A yard or outdoor space at a school, sometimes with sports or recreational equipment, where children can play (usually under supervision) when they are not receiving lessons in class.

Playgroup (education)
An organized activity group for pre-school age children (also known as a playschool) in the mornings or afternoons, arranged on a private basis and often organized by the children's mothers (but outside the formal structure of a nursery school, whether state or private).

Poet Laureate, the (arts)
The honorary title of the poet appointed for life to the royal household by the sovereign. The poet may write occasional verse for royal or state occasions such as a coronation, royal wedding or birthday, or state funeral. The present Poet Laureate is Ted Hughes.

Polaris missile, the (military)
See **Independent nuclear deterrent**.

Police, the (law)
Britain has no one national police force, but 52 regional forces

covering the country. London is catered for by the Metropolitan Police Force (with its headquarters at New Scotland Yard) and the City (of London) force. The British police are not armed, except on special occasions, and they perform a number of duties in the community such as investigating crimes, arresting people, protecting citizens and property, and controlling traffic. The police forces are under the operational control of a chief constable for the region and under the supervision of a civilian police committee of the local government authority. Any complaints against them may be made to the Police Complaints Authority. Their powers are controlled by codes of conduct and practice, and their professional interests are looked after by the Police Federation.

Poll tax, the (finance)
See **Community charge**.

Polling booths (politics)
Enclosed or private sections of a polling station in which a voter secretly registers his or her vote on a ballot paper during an election, such as a by-election or general election.

Polling day (politics)
A Thursday (also known as election day) which is set aside for electors to register their votes at polling stations in an election, such as a by-election or general election. The final nationwide results of a general election are usually known on Friday, although early results in some places are declared on Thursday evening and others follow throughout the night.

Polling station (politics)
A public building, such as a hall or a school, which serves as a place where voters can cast their votes on election day, and which usually opens from 7.00 am to 10.00 pm.

Polytechnics (education)
The 34 institutions of higher education in England and Wales (and 13 similar institutions in Scotland) that supply a large number of vocational and academic courses at degree and diploma levels, which may be part-time or full-time. They were once closely tied to their local government councils, but are now independent corporate bodies, and since 1992 have been allowed to apply for (and most have been granted) university status.

Polytechnics' Central Admission System (education)
See **Universities' Central Council on Admissions (UCCA)**.

Pools, the (sport and leisure)
A popular gambling activity, organized by private commercial companies, in which individuals bet on the results of professional football matches each Saturday in the season, by marking a pools coupon (or form) with the predicted results and posting it to the pools companies. It is a relatively cheap pastime, but large amounts of money can be won.

Popular papers (the populars) (media)
Daily or Sunday national newspapers, mostly in tabloid form, with big headlines, brief news reports, many photographs, personal stories, sporting pages, entertainment features and bingo games. Their style, content and language are intended for quick and easy reading by largely working- or lower middle-class readers. National daily popular papers are the *Daily Express*, the *Daily Mirror*, the *Daily Mail, The Star, The Sun* and *Today*. National Sunday popular papers are the *Sunday Express*, the *Mail on Sunday*, the *Sunday Mirror*, the *News of the World*, the *Sunday Sport* and the *People*.

Popular vote, the (politics)
The total number of votes actually cast by the electorate in an election. Under the British electoral system a government may achieve an overall majority of seats in the House of Commons with a minority of the popular vote, that is, less than the votes awarded to the opposition parties counted together.

Port of London Authority, the (PLA) (transport)
The independent body (or public trust) that has organized London's port and docks since 1910 but which, after the redevelopment of the London Docklands in the 1980s, now mainly manages the Tilbury Docks east of London and dredges the River Thames. It was, however, responsible for the construction of the Thames Barrier. Similar bodies manage other major ports in Britain, although some are now run by nationalized groups or organized by local authorities.

Positive vetting (PV) (government)
The official investigation of the personal backgrounds of government and military employees who work in sensitive or security jobs, with the aim of evaluating their suitability for their positions.

Post Office, the (PO) (communications)
The national postal service and state corporation which has a monopoly on, and is in charge of, the collection and delivery of letters

and parcels through the Royal Mail, and which manages other services such as the National Savings Bank and the sale of postage stamps through its nationwide network of post offices. Postmen/women deliver letters once or twice daily and parcels once a day to private and public buildings (except on Sundays and bank holidays, and with only one delivery on Saturdays).

Postal vote (politics)
The electoral procedure whereby a registered voter who is unable to be in his or her parliamentary constituency during a general or by-election is allowed to cast a personal vote and to send it to the constituency by post.

Postcode (communications)
The last element of all British postal addresses, consisting of a set of letters and figures (such as PO19 1TS) which provides detailed identification of the postal area and which is used by the Post Office to sort mail electronically.

Postgraduate (education)
A student (also known as a graduate or graduate student) who has finished a programme of study at an institution of higher education (usually for a first degree) and who continues studying for a higher degree or diploma.

Pound (sterling), the (finance)
The basic unit of the British currency, which now takes the form of a pound coin and is divided into 100 pence. It is written as a £, which is placed before the number of pounds, such as £10 (10 pounds).

Poverty line, the (society and finance)
A common term to describe the position where a person's total income falls below the basic subsistence or social security level, or where it is below half the national average wage, or where it is under the European Community 'decency level'.

Power-Gen (science and commerce)
See **Electricity supplies**.

Power-sharing (politics)
A proposed solution to the problems of Northern Ireland in which the majority Protestants would share political power in the province with the minority Roman Catholics by some form of weighted voting or proportional system. All attempts to achieve this on a permanent basis have failed.

Precedent (government and law)
A solution for a particular problem, or a decision in a specific case, which can be used in similar situations in the future. It is an important device in British governmental, legal and administrative institutions.

Prefab (housing)
A house, normally on ground level, which is constructed of ready-made (or prefabricated) units, usually of concrete.

Prefect (education)
A senior boy or girl in some secondary schools (both state and independent) who is appointed to a position of limited authority, and who may be responsible for certain aspects of a particular class (such as discipline) under the supervision of the class teacher.

Preference shares (finance)
Company shares which have priority over ordinary shares when dividends on trading profits are declared and paid to shareholders by the company.

Premium (finance)
The amount of money paid periodically (usually annually) on financial policies (such as insurance) which is necessary to maintain the policy.

Premium (Savings) Bonds (finance)
A form of government lottery created in 1956. Bonds (or legal certificates of a loan), on which no interest is paid, are issued by the Treasury and sold to the public through the Post Office (PO). The bonds are then entered in monthly and weekly draws (or competitions) for cash prizes of various amounts, which are tax-free.

Preparatory (prep) school (education)
A fee-paying school in the independent education sector for children usually between the ages of 7 and 13 for boys and 7 and 11 for girls, with the aim of preparing pupils for independent secondary schools. Some are boarding schools, some are for boys or girls only, and some constitute the junior part of a public school. Many pupils transfer from a preparatory school to a public school by successfully passing the Common Entrance examination. A private pre-preparatory school will often prepare children aged 5 to 7 for entry to a preparatory school.

Prescription (medicine)
A written note filled out by a doctor or dentist under the state NHS system for a patient's medicines or medical aids, which the patient will have prepared by a chemist for a standard charge. Some 70 per cent of patients receive free prescription services, such as children under 16, pregnant mothers, OAPs and those on income support and family credit. Private patients also receive prescriptions from their doctor, but must pay the full cost of their medicine themselves.

Presiding officer (politics)
An individual, usually a local government official, who supervises the activities of a polling station on election day during a by-election or general election.

Press, the (media)
A common collective term for newspapers, journalists and the overall organization and management of the newspaper industry.

Press Association, the (PA) (media)
An independent and influential news agency, established in 1868, which supplies a news service and details of national affairs to newspapers throughout Britain, the BBC, ITN and other customers who subscribe to its service.

Press Complaints Commission, the (PCC) (media)
An independent body originally founded by newspaper owners in 1953 as the Press Council to preserve the freedom and standards of the British press. Now known as the PCC, it assesses complaints made by the public about the activities and reporting of newspapers and magazines, which must publish its findings.

Pressure group (society)
An independent organization, similar to lobbyists and interest groups, which puts pressure on government and other bodies to achieve a particular end or interest, such as greater state support for OAPs and one-parent families.

Prestel (media)
See **Teletext**.

Prevention of Terrorism Act, the (law)
A 1974 Act of Parliament which empowers the police and other state authorities to refuse the admission to Britain of any person who has connections with terrorism in Northern Ireland or to expel

Northern Irish citizens from the mainland to Northern Ireland. It also enables the police to arrest people suspected of being involved in terrorism, whether in Northern Ireland or the rest of Britain, and to hold them in custody for up to 96 hours without charge.

Primary school (education)
A state school for children aged 5–11, often divided into infant and junior stages, after which they proceed automatically to a secondary school. Some pupils in this age group, however, may attend a first school or middle school, depending on local educational organization.

Prime Minister, the (PM) (government)
The head of Her Majesty's government, who is appointed by the monarch, sits in the House of Commons, presides over the Cabinet, chooses government ministers, is the head of the Civil Service, and is responsible for the country's domestic and foreign policies. He or she also recommends other legal, religious and state appointments to the sovereign.

Prince (royalty)
The title automatically given at birth to the sons of the sovereign and their sons, as in Prince Charles and his son Prince William. It is also usually granted to the husband of a queen, as in Prince Philip the husband of Queen Elizabeth II.

Prince Consort (royalty)
The courtesy, but not automatic, title given to the husband of a reigning queen by that queen. It was last held by Prince Albert (1819–61), the husband of Queen Victoria.

Prince (Princess) of Wales, the (royalty)
The title of Prince of Wales is traditionally conferred on the sovereign's eldest son, and therefore heir to the throne, by the sovereign. The current Prince of Wales is Prince Charles who was invested, following historical precedent, as Prince of Wales at Caernarfon Castle in North Wales. In 1981 he married Lady Diana Spencer, who automatically became the Princess of Wales. Their two sons (William and Henry) rank second and third in succession to the throne.

Princess (royalty)
The title bestowed automatically at birth on the daughters of the sovereign, as in Princess Anne, and on the daughters of a prince or princess (unless it is revoked).

Princess Royal (royalty)
An honour awarded to the eldest or only daughter of a British monarch, which is not an official title or rank. Queen Elizabeth bestowed it on her daughter, Princess Anne, in 1987.

Private bill (government)
A bill introduced into Parliament which concerns a particular local or individual interest (such as a measure required by a local authority, a private individual or a nationalized industry to carry on specific work). It then goes through a similar process to the creation of an Act of Parliament, although most of the work is done in committee, the proposers have to prove their case, and opposing views must be heard. It is distinct from a public bill, and should not be confused with a private member's bill.

Private health (medicine)
The general term to describe the private health sector which provides medical facilities outside the state National Health Service (NHS) in private hospitals and clinics, and by doctors and consultants giving a private service. Individuals pay for their treatment either out of income or from private health insurance policies.

Private income (finance)
Money or income (also known as private wealth or means) which does not derive from regular paid employment but from unearned sources such as investment or inheritance.

Private limited company (Ltd) (finance)
A business that is not a public limited company (plc), and which cannot offer to sell its shares to the general public. It puts Ltd (Limited) after its name to show that it is a private limited company, meaning that its shareholders are legally liable, in the event of collapse, only for the amount of their paid-up shares. The majority of companies in Britain are small private limited companies, although some large national concerns are private for legal and financial reasons.

Private member (government)
An MP in the House of Commons who is not a member of the government (such as a minister) or of the Opposition Shadow Cabinet (as a Shadow minister), and so is an ordinary backbencher.

Private member's bill (government)
A public bill introduced into the House of Commons by a private member (or MP) after a ballot among MPs to decide which bills

will be introduced. It frequently reflects a personal interest of the
MP, but most bills do not proceed far in the Commons (and become
Acts) due to lack of support and time.

Private patient (medicine)
A patient who chooses not to obtain medical treatment on the state
NHS system but who pays for it, either from personal income or
through private health insurance schemes run by a specialist medical
insurance company such as the British United Provident Association
(BUPA).

Private practice (medicine)
A doctor's medical surgery or clinic for private patients, and where
treatment is paid for by the individual patient or by medical
insurance.

Private school (education)
An alternative term for a fee-paying school in the independent
school sector, such as a preparatory, public or other independent
school. Such schools are outside the state (non-fee-paying) school
sector, and they usually have charitable legal status.

Private sector (commerce)
That sector of the British economy which consists of privately
owned businesses and services, as opposed to the state-owned public
sector, and which accounts for over two-thirds of the national
economy.

Privatization (government)
The political and economic policy of the Conservative government
since 1979 whereby publicly owned state concerns and industries
have been transferred to private sector ownership, mostly by the
sale of shares in the new companies, such as British Telecom (BT)
and British Airways (BA).

Privy Council, the (PC) (government and royalty)
Historically the private advisory council of the sovereign, composed
of close associates at the court. Apart from its important Judicial
Committee, the council's chief role now is to advise the sovereign
to formally approve government decisions (orders in council). All
Cabinet ministers are automatically members of the Privy Council
(Privy Councillors), and the sovereign may appoint eminent people
in Britain and Commonwealth countries as members. There are
currently about 400 Privy Councillors, but a full meeting of the

council is held only on the death of a sovereign or in special constitutional situations.

Privy Purse, the (royalty)
The income from the royal estates, which is used to pay the costs and expenditure of the sovereign as monarch, and not when he or she is performing the duties of head of state, the expenses of which are paid by the Civil List.

Privy Seal, the (government)
An insignia (or national badge) which is embossed on or attached to certain less important royal (and government) documents that do not require the Great Seal.

Probate (law)
The legal procedure of proving in the High Court in England and Wales that a will is genuine, and that property and money left in the will can safely be distributed to the beneficiaries. Probate also occurs when no will has been made (intestacy), but the estate still has to be determined or settled.

Probation (law)
An element of the state penal system in which a court orders that a convicted criminal be placed under the supervision of a probation officer from the government probation service for a period of up to three years instead of going to prison. The intention of this non-custodial sentence is to re-establish the offender in society. He or she is on probation, which means that if further offences are committed the person will receive a custodial sentence.

Procurator-fiscal (PF) (law)
An officer of the sheriff court in Scotland who serves as a public prosecutor in the same way as the Crown Prosecution Service in England and Wales. He or she also performs the same functions as an English and Welsh coroner.

Promenade Concerts, the (arts)
Annual summer concerts of mainly classical music (known commonly as the Proms), first held in 1895, now sponsored by the BBC and held at the Albert Hall, London. The concerts are a national institution and popular with people of all ages. The Last Night of the Proms is the occasion on which patriotic music and songs are traditionally performed.

Proportional representation (PR) (politics)
The electoral system in which a political party obtains representa-

tives in an election in proportion to the number of people who actually voted for it, in contrast to the British first-past-the-post system. There has been a demand in some quarters in Britain (such as the Liberal Democrats) for the adoption of the PR system, but the Conservatives are opposed and the Labour Party is divided.

Prorogation (government)
The formal ending of a session of Parliament by the sovereign on the advice of the Prime Minister. The life of a five-year Parliament is divided into sessions of about one year each.

Prosecution (law)
The official representative of the state in criminal matters. The Crown Prosecution Service (CPS) in England and Wales conducts cases against accused persons in the name of the Crown or state. In Scotland the job is done by the Crown Office and the Procurator-Fiscal Service, and in Northern Ireland by the police and the Director of Public Prosecutions.

Prospective parliamentary candidate (politics)
A politician who has been chosen by a constituency party to represent it as its candidate in a forthcoming parliamentary general or by-election in that constituency.

Protestant (religion)
A member of a religious church or group which historically did not accept the rule, doctrine and practices of the Roman Catholic Church, such as the Church of England.

Provinces, the (geography)
A general term to refer to those areas in Britain which lie outside London. See also **Home Counties**.

Provost (education and local government)
1. The executive head of some institutions of higher education and schools, particularly in the independent sector. 2. The leading local government representative in some Scottish towns, similar to a mayor in England and Wales.

Proxy vote (politics and society)
An electoral system, usually at a by-election or general election, that allows an individual to cast a vote for another person who cannot be physically present during the election. The proxy must vote in accordance with the other person's wishes and formal permission must be obtained before the procedure is employed. Proxy

voting may also be used in other situations outside politics, such as at company meetings.

Public bill (government)
A bill introduced, generally by the government, into either of the two Houses of Parliament which, after the various procedural stages, will become an Act of Parliament. It is a bill that affects national and public activities, and is distinguished from a private bill.

Public house (pub) (society)
A building with a distinctive name sign outside, also known as an inn and commonly as one's local, where alcoholic drinks and food are sold for consumption on the premises to persons over 18, and which may now open from 11.00 am to 11.00 pm, but to which children under 14 are not generally admitted. Pubs are a traditional feature of British towns and villages, and vary widely in age and style. For many people they function as social clubs, and have various recreational facilities, such as music and darts. Most pubs are owned by a particular brewery and are known as tied houses, which means that only certain beers from specified breweries are sold. Others are known as free houses, and are able to receive their supplies from a number of brewers.

Public inquiries (law and government)
See **Administrative inquiries**.

Public Lending Right (PLR) (law)
A method, introduced by the Conservative government in 1984, by which variable sums of money are paid from public finances to those authors whose books are borrowed from public libraries by members of the public.

Public limited company (plc) (finance)
A company whose shares are offered for sale to the public on the (London) Stock Exchange, and which is not a private limited company (Ltd). Such companies are usually large industrial or commercial enterprises and must have the words public limited company (or plc) after their name. The liability of shareholders is limited to the number of their paid-up shares.

Public opinion polls (society)
Questions asked of selected samples of the public on specific topics which are then used to gauge, in percentage terms, national reactions to a wide range of matters. The polls are professionally con-

ducted by institutions such as MORI (Market and Opinion Research International) and Marplan (Market Research Plan), and have proved very accurate. The results are usually published in national newspapers, which may have commissioned a particular poll themselves.

Public Record Office, the (PRO) (government)
The national depository partly in central London but mostly now at Kew in West London that holds official state records and historic documents, including those of the courts of law and most government departments. It is open to researchers and to the public.

Public schools (education)
A group of some 200 independent fee-paying secondary schools in England which provide education for pupils from 13 (sometimes 11) to 18, such as Eton, Harrow, Westminster and Winchester for boys and Roedean and Cheltenham Ladies' College for girls. Many of them are ancient foundations on a boarding basis, with a reputation for high academic standards. Some take only boys or only girls, but many have now become coeducational. A public school is usually defined by its membership of the Headmasters' Conference and the adjective 'public' is thought to derive from the fact that pupils could enter the school from anywhere in England and not just from areas close to the school. The term is also sometimes used for a school in Scotland that is financed by the state and is non-fee-paying unlike the English public schools.

Public sector (government)
The group of industries and services in Britain which are owned and managed by the state (amounting to under one-third of the national economy), in distinction to the private sector.

Public sector borrowing requirement (PSBR) (finance)
The money that the government has to borrow from the public to make up for the shortfall it receives from official revenue and income. The additional finance is usually raised by selling government stock, securities and national savings.

Public service broadcasting (media)
A concept historically applied to the BBC, which has seen its national role as educating, informing and entertaining the public, who finance its services through the television licence fee.

Punter (sport and leisure)
Generally an individual who gambles on the results of horse-races,

greyhound-races and other sporting events. It has recently also come to mean a client or customer in many different situations.

Pupil (education)
The term generally and traditionally applied to schoolchildren, rather than the word student which is used in further and higher education.

Pupillage (law)
The one-year period of practical training with an established barrister that a student barrister has to complete after passing professional examinations and before being able to practise as a fully qualified barrister.

Q

Quakers, the (religion)
The common name for the Society of Friends, a Protestant Christian organization established in England in 1668 by George Fox (and now a worldwide movement), with equality for all its members. Quakers have no ordained ministers, outward observance of sacraments, or conventionally organized religious services. They gather together for periods of silent meditation and 'meetings' to which anyone can make a contribution. Quakers are well known for their pacifism, charitable and educational work, and support for the oppressed and underprivileged.

Quality newspapers (the qualities) (media)
Quality newspapers are those daily or Sunday national newspapers which are targeted at the educated reader and which are contrasted with the mass-circulation popular papers. They have detailed news reports, informative commentaries, in-depth editorials, topical articles by specialists, reviews of the arts and literature, and considerable upmarket advertising. The national daily quality papers are the *Daily Telegraph*, the *Financial Times*, the *Guardian*, the *Independent* and *The Times*. The national Sunday quality papers are the *Sunday Telegraph*, the *Observer*, the *Sunday Times* and the *Independent on Sunday*, which also have colour supplements consisting of feature articles, a range of advertisements, and photographs.

Quango (government)
An abbreviation for 'quasi-autonomous non-governmental organizations', first established in the 1970s. A quango is largely financed by central government, but functions separately from it. It is a public agency, such as the British Council, the Arts Council (ACGB) and the Commission for Racial Equality (CRE), which acts in an advisory, academic or judicial capacity in areas of public life. Some quangos have now been abolished and the future of others is uncertain.

Quarter days (society)
The days which coincide with the four quarters of the calendar year

in Britain, and which have traditionally been associated with ancient religious festivals. These latter references are not in general use today, but they approximate to the dates in the year (a quarter) when regular payments and bills like rent, insurance premiums and interest become payable, that is, at the end of March, June, September and December, although these can vary.

Quarterlies, the (media)
Magazines and other periodicals which are published on a quarterly basis, that is, four times a calendar year.

Queen (royalty)
A female sovereign, currently Queen Elizabeth II, who formally holds positions as head of state, head of the legal system, commander-in-chief of the armed forces and head of the Church of England, among others. She is involved in governmental activities such as the summoning, prorogation and dissolution of Parliament, and parliamentary bills must be given the Royal Assent before they can finally become law. She awards honours on the advice of the Prime Minister, but some can be decided personally. She invites the leader of a party winning a general election to form a government and thus appoints the Prime Minister. The Queen has the formal power to declare war and make peace, recognize foreign states and governments, and conclude treaties, although these prerogative powers now rest with the sitting government. She appoints government ministers, judges, diplomats and bishops in the Church of England to their offices, and is able to grant a royal pardon to convicted criminals.

Queen Mother, the (royalty)
The title given to the surviving wife of a deceased king, such as the present Queen Elizabeth the Queen Mother (widow of King George VI).

Queen-in-Parliament, the (government)
The correct constitutional name for the British legislative system. The House of Commons, the House of Lords and formally the monarch constitute Parliament as a law-creating body, and the activities of the Commons and the Lords are carried out in the Queen's name.

Queen's Bench Division (of the High Court), the (law)
One of the three divisions of the High Court of Justice in England and Wales, presided over by the Lord Chief Justice. It mainly

determines civil cases such as actions for damages for breach of
contract and tort (negligence matters) and the recovery of land or
goods.

Queen's birthday, the (royalty)
Either the date of the personal birthday of Queen Elizabeth II (21
April), when no special activities take place, or of her Official
Birthday, on the second Saturday in June, which is marked by
Trooping the Colour on Horse Guards Parade in London, and the
announcement of the Birthday Honours. Neither of these occasions
is a bank holiday.

Queen's (King's) counsel (QC or KC) (law)
A senior barrister, originally appointed by the monarch but now
on the recommendation of the Lord Chancellor, and a promotional
step towards a judgeship. The appointment is known as 'taking silk'
and such barristers, who argue important legal cases, wear silk
gowns when appearing in court and are assisted by junior barristers.

Queen's (King's) Speech, the (government)
The speech, actually written by government ministers, but which is
read from the throne in the House of Lords to the assembled
Parliament by the sovereign at the opening of a new session of
Parliament. The speech contains an outline of the government's
programme and policies for the coming session.

Question time (government)
The sessions each day of the week in the House of Commons when
the Prime Minister (Tuesdays and Thursdays) and other ministers
in the government (Mondays, Tuesdays, Wednesdays and
Thursdays) are subject to both oral and written questions from
MPs. It can be a testing time at which reputations may be made
or broken.

Quoted shares (finance)
The shares of public limited companies which are dealt with
(quoted) on the (London) Stock Exchange, the prices of which can
go up as well as down. Also referred to as listed shares.

R

Race meeting (sport and leisure)
The occasion when horses or greyhounds compete on particular racecourses at specific times of the day or evening, such as the 2.30 race at Kempton (a horse-race).

Race Relations Act, the (law)
Britain has had a long and varied history of settlement and immigration from overseas which has resulted in many ethnic and racial minority groups in its population, particularly since the late 1950s. The problems of minorities are partly covered by social welfare programmes and their legal rights by the Race Relations Act 1976, which created the Commission for Racial Equality (CRE) to serve as a body dealing with race relations activities.

Radio 1 (media)
The national BBC radio channel which supplies a 21-hour daily service consisting largely of popular music and news flashes (usually on the hour).

Radio 2 (media)
The national BBC radio channel which supplies a 24-hour daily service of light entertainment and variety shows, music and sports programmes, with hourly news bulletins.

Radio 3 (media)
The national BBC radio channel which supplies a 17-hour daily broadcasting service largely of classical music, but also drama, poetry, short stories, talks and some programmes for the Open University.

Radio 4 (media)
The national BBC radio channel which supplies an 18-hour daily service of news and current affairs, in addition to drama productions, comedy shows, educational series, documentaries and panel games. It also carries parliamentary coverage and live reports of major state or public events.

Radio 5 (media)
A national radio channel of the BBC, launched in 1990. It is

devoted mainly to sport and educational programmes, but may be either changed or phased out in the near future.

Radio Authority, the (media)
The Radio Authority has had responsibility for local and national independent radio since 1991, awards licences to independent radio companies, and supervises their activities. In the early 1990s it allocated licences to three new national independent radio services, the first of which was awarded in 1991 to Classic FM, which plays mainly popular classical music.

Radio Times, the (RT) (media)
A BBC magazine, established in 1923, which publishes the television and radio programme schedules of the BBC, ITC and Radio Authority for each week. The magazine, which also includes topical features and photographs, now competes with *TV Times* to provide this scheduling service.

Railways (transport)
The world's first scheduled passenger service was established on the Stockton and Darlington railway in northern England in 1825. The Liverpool and Manchester railway in 1829 was the first to operate a scheduled service according to a timetable, and using railway stations. Originally the British railway companies and systems were privately owned, but were nationalized in 1948. Today most railways and their services in Britain are state-owned and operated by British Rail, which will be privatized by the Conservative government.

Ranger Guides, the (sport and leisure)
See **Guides Association**.

Rates (finance and government)
Historically these were taxes paid to the local authority by landowners and the owners of property. They were based on a locally devised rateable value of property and helped to pay the costs of local government services. The old rates were abolished in 1989–90 and replaced by the community charge (poll tax), which was then also abolished to be replaced in 1993–4 by a new council tax based on property values and an assumed household of two people. This tax is calculated annually by the appropriate local authority and paid by local homeowners.

Ratings, the (media)
A classification system whereby television programmes are rated

according to their popularity with viewers, and based on the number of people who watch the programmes. It is an important indication for the BBC and independent television companies of how their programmes are being received by the public.

Rebate (finance)
A percentage amount of money which is deducted from a total bill, and for which an individual qualifies on some ground, such as a low income or old age pensioner status.

Receiver (law)
An individual such as an accountant (a professionally qualified financial expert) who is officially appointed to supervise the property or business of a bankrupt or insane person, with the duty to pay off debts and usually to dispose of the assets of a company.

Recess (government)
The period of time, such as the summer holiday or between the ending of one Parliament and the beginning of a new one, when Parliament is closed and little if any parliamentary business is carried on.

Recorder (law)
A qualified barrister or solicitor of 10 years' seniority who is appointed by the Crown on the advice of the Lord Chancellor to serve as a part-time judge in a crown court and county court in England and Wales.

Rector (religion and education)
1. Another name for an ordained clergyman or priest in the Church of England who is in charge of a (usually large) parish or group of parishes. 2. The head of some schools and institutions of higher education.

Red Ensign, the (transport)
The traditional flag flown by all Merchant Navy ships (known commonly as the Red Duster), which has a red background with the Union Flag (or Jack) in the top quarter next to the flagpole.

Red Hand of Ulster, the (society)
The badge of Northern Ireland, which appears in the middle of flags as an upright red hand cut off at the wrist.

Redbrick universities (education)
A number of English universities which were established in the late nineteenth or early twentieth centuries, usually in major industrial

cities such as Leeds or Manchester. Such universities were frequently constructed of red brick, and were often contrasted negatively to the architecture of Oxford and Cambridge Universities.

Redundancy (employment)
Occurs when people lose their jobs, either because their workplace is closing down, or because there is a fundamental reorganization of work practices. The employees can claim a redundancy payment based on their age and length of employment if they have worked there for at least two years.

Re-examination (law)
A process in a court of law whereby a witness can be recalled to the witness stand to be examined or questioned again on evidence which has already been covered.

Referendum (government)
The process by which voters can directly influence the making of laws and national policy. In Britain it is a vote of the electorate on a specific item, but has been used only on very limited occasions, such as the first in British history in 1975 on Britain's continuing membership of the EC, and by Scottish and Welsh voters on devolution proposals in the late 1970s. Referendums in Britain are not usually legally binding on Parliament.

Refresher course (education)
Courses usually at an educational institution which are intended to bring students or employees up to date on the latest developments in their particular subject or area of work.

Regent (royalty)
The person appointed to act on behalf of a reigning monarch if the sovereign is incapable of performing his or her duties, is absent from Britain, or under 18. A regent would usually operate through the Privy Council.

Regina (Rex) (law)
The Latin term for queen (rex for king) officially employed by the state prosecution in criminal proceedings during the reign of a queen ('Regina v Smith') or king ('Rex v Smith') to illustrate that legally the sovereign (representing the state) is the formal prosecutor in criminal cases.

Region (government and society)
A general term to refer to a specific area of the country, and which

may be applied to local functions such as health, gas and electricity services. In Scotland and Northern Ireland it is the local government unit equivalent to a county in England and Wales.

Regional health authority (RHA) (medicine)
England, because of its greater size and population, has an additional level of local health authority above that of district health authority (DHA), often based on a teaching hospital. The RHA is responsible for regional planning, resource allocation, major capital building work and certain specialized hospital services.

Register of voters (government)
The record of registered voters eligible to vote either in a parliamentary constituency or local government area, with their names and addresses. It is also known as an electoral register and is kept in local government offices, and the local authority is responsible for keeping it up-to-date.

Register office (government)
A local government office (sometimes called a registry office) where civil or state (non-religious) marriages are performed, and where all the births, marriages and deaths in the local area have to be registered and recorded in registers. The person in administrative charge of the office is known as a registrar.

Registrar (law)
1. A lawyer, usually a solicitor, who often has administrative charge of a county court and High Court branch in England and Wales, and who assists the judge and decides some civil cases. 2. The public official who is in charge of a register office.

Registration number (transport)
A new motor vehicle is given an official number by the Driver and Vehicle Licensing Agency (DVLA) when it is first registered by an owner, which is displayed on number plates at the back and front of a car or a lorry, and at the back of a motor-cycle.

Registry (religion)
A room in a church in which the official records of the church, often centuries old, are stored, such as registers of baptisms, marriages and burials.

Regulator (government)
The independent body (such as Ofgas, Oftel, Ofwat and Offer) or person appointed by the government to oversee and hear complaints

relating to the new privatized industries (such as prices and the quality of services), and to make recommendations.

Relate (society)
An umbrella voluntary body (known previously as the National Marriage Guidance Council) to which are affiliated (or connected) local marriage guidance centres that give advice and help with personal and family problems.

Remand (law)
The legal term for a court's decision either to commit a defendant to custody, or to release a defendant on bail, until the next stage in criminal proceedings. A defendant may be remanded in custody (in a prison, a police station or remand centre) for a period of eight days. Further remands, however, can be made, so that the person, still legally assumed to be innocent, may be held for many months.

Remand centre (law)
Young defendants up to 17, awaiting trial and not granted bail, are committed to one of seven remand centres in Britain where they are detained until further proceedings are taken in their case, or while awaiting trial.

Remembrance Day (society)
See **Albert Hall**, **Armistice Day** and **Cenotaph**.

Rent (finance)
The amount of money which a person (tenant) pays to a property owner (landlord/landlady) in exchange for living in the property. This applies in both the private and public rented housing sectors. The term is also used where a tenant hires commercial premises from a landlord in order to carry on a business.

Rent Acts (government and law)
Legislation (such as the Rent Act 1977) which was intended to make conditions more secure and rents more stable for tenants in rented accommodation. These measures led to a reduction in the number of privately rented properties in Britain because landlords were unable to charge market rents and could not easily dismiss tenants. The situation has changed recently with the introduction of short tenancies from which private tenants can be dismissed at the end of the tenancy.

Repertory theatre (arts)
A permanent local theatre company that produces plays from a

fixed programme or performs a specific number of productions in a season. There are many such theatres throughout Britain and they have been traditionally seen as the training ground for actors and actresses.

Report stage (government)
After the second reading of a bill in the House of Commons and the resulting committee stage, the legislative process continues to the report stage during which further amendments to the bill may be considered.

Repossession (housing and finance)
When a home owner is unable to keep up the repayments of a loan on the house to a lender (such as a building society), the latter takes over the property and the resident loses the home. The lender forecloses on (brings to an end) the loan.

Representation (law and government)
The situation where one person stands in the place of another, such as a lawyer who represents (speaks on behalf of) a client in a court of law, and an MP who serves in a representative capacity for all of his or her constituents in the House of Commons.

Restrictive practice (commerce and employment)
Any commercial or professional practice which restricts the choice of consumers and others, and which is against the public interest, such as the employment methods of some trade unions and professional bodies, or a business agreement to sell goods only to specified customers.

Retail Price Index, the (RPI) (finance)
The average prices of certain selected commodities calculated on a monthly basis which form the estimation for the level of national price inflation in the economy (given in percentage terms).

Retailer (commerce)
A shopkeeper who sells goods for a specified price to a customer. Unlike a wholesaler, the goods are not intended for resale.

Retirement age (employment)
The age at which employed people normally retire from their jobs in Britain (currently 65 for men and 60 for women), and receive a state pension. Individuals may, however, retire earlier, in which case they do not receive the state pension until they reach the age of 65/60, or later. Discussions are continuing at present on how the state retirement ages can be equalized between men and women.

Returning officer (government)
The local government official (often the mayor) who formally presides over the election process in a by-, local or general election, and who announces the results.

Reuters (media)
The main British news agency which supplies information to media organizations worldwide, originally established in 1851. It became a public limited company (plc) in 1984, and sells its shares on the (London) Stock Exchange.

Revenue (finance)
Refers to money which a company or government receives from a range of sources, such as profits and taxation.

Reverend, the (Rev.) (religion)
The formal title of an ordained clergyman in the Church of England and in many of the Free Churches, and by which he is addressed, as in the spoken 'the Reverend John Smith' or the written 'the Rev. John Smith'.

Revised Version, the (RV) (religion)
A modernized revision of the Authorized Version of the Bible (the King James Bible), prepared from 1881 to 1895, and used in many churches in preference to the earlier translation.

Right of audience (law)
The professional right which a lawyer has to appear before a particular court of law on a client's behalf. In England and Wales at present only barristers have the right to appear in all courts, and solicitors are restricted to the lower courts. But this situation is due to change and qualified solicitor-advocates will be allowed to appear in the higher courts.

Right of centre (politics)
A term to describe a moderate political ideology and set of policies which is near the middle of more extreme opposing points of view from the left and right of the political spectrum.

Right Reverend, the (Rt Rev.) (religion)
The formal and official title of a bishop in the Church of England, as in the written style of 'The Rt Rev. the (Lord) Bishop of Durham'.

Right-to-buy (housing)
Legislation introduced by the Conservative government in 1980 which allows tenants in council or public housing to buy at below-

market prices the houses or flats that they are renting from the local council, and in which they have lived for at least two years.

Right wing (politics)
A term to describe a political position opposite to a left-wing (more socialist) point of view, which in Britain is generally applied to the Conservative Party as a whole, although the party does have its right and left wings.

Robbery (law)
Robbery is theft (the unlawful taking away of another person's property) accompanied by force or the threat of force.

Roman Catholic Church, the (religion)
After the conversion of most parts of the British Isles to Christianity in the fifth and sixth centuries, the dominant Christian Church was the Roman Catholic Church and its religious and legal influence increased in succeeding centuries. But after the Reformation and Henry VIII's break with the supremacy of the Church of Rome in the sixteenth century, the new national Church of England gradually became Protestant and the Roman Catholic Church was effectively destroyed for a period. The Church was eventually restored with full religious freedom for its members by the end of the nineteenth century, although the offices of sovereign, regent and Lord Chancellor are still closed to Catholics. The Church is currently the second largest in Britain after the Church of England in terms of potential members, with an active membership of some 2.2 million.

Round Britain Cycle Race, the (sport and leisure)
The biggest annual international cycle race for amateurs and professionals in Britain established in 1951. It covers a road circuit throughout Britain of some 1,500 miles (2,419 km) and lasts for some 14 days. It is sponsored by a prominent commercial company (currently Kellogg's).

Rounders (sport and leisure)
A ball game popular with children at school or at home, in which the players attempt to hit with a small wooden bat a ball thrown to them by a bowler. Depending on how far they have hit the ball, they attempt to run round four bases before the ball is returned to the bowler. If a full round is not completed the player must stop at one of the bases, and can continue only when the next player strikes the ball.

Royal Academy (of Arts), the (RA) (arts)
An independent association of artists and the oldest society (1768) in Britain to concentrate on the fine arts. It is based in London and holds a well known annual summer exhibition of contemporary art.

Royal Academy of Dramatic Art, the (RADA) (arts)
The influential and well known London drama school, established in 1904, that trains professional actors and actresses for the stage in Britain.

Royal Academy of Music, the (RAM) (arts and education)
The oldest (1822) college of advanced musical training in England, based in London, which awards degrees and diplomas to students.

Royal Air Force, the (RAF) (military)
The youngest of the three British armed forces, officially established in 1918. It is under the control of the Department of Defence, and its total personnel of men and women is some 88,000, although this will be gradually reduced.

Royal and Ancient, the (R and A) (sport and leisure)
An old (1754) and important golf club in St Andrews, Scotland (Royal and Ancient Golf Club of St Andrews), which is an international golfing centre acknowledged widely as the home of golf.

Royal Assent, the (government)
The formal acceptance by the sovereign of a parliamentary bill, and the final stage in its passage through Parliament, as a result of which it becomes an Act of Parliament and law.

Royal Automobile Club, the (RAC) (transport)
One of two main bodies (with the AA) for motorists in Britain, established in 1897. It provides its members with technical advice and help (including assistance with breakdowns on the road), and publishes travel guides and motoring books.

Royal Ballet, the (arts)
Britain's national ballet company, established in London in 1931. Its repertoire includes nineteenth-century classical and English works and it performs mainly at the Royal Opera House, Covent Garden, London, but also tours throughout Britain and the world. It now has a permanent branch in Birmingham (the Birmingham Royal Ballet).

Royal British Legion, the (RBL) (society and military)
A national association of British ex-servicemen/women and current members of the armed forces, established in 1921. It aims to commemorate all servicemen/women who have died in armed conflicts and provides aid for ex-service personnel and their families. Its best known activity is the manufacture and sale of artificial poppies on days near to Poppy Day (Armistice Day).

Royal Charter (government)
The sovereign through the Privy Council grants charters (or permission to operate) to a range of institutions such as universities and the BBC, which give them legal status and independence, and describe the regulations under which they function.

Royal College of Art, the (RCA) (education)
A postgraduate art college in London, established in 1837, that provides professional courses for art students and awards higher and research degrees.

Royal College of Music, the (RCM) (education)
A leading musical college in London, established in 1883, that provides training for students who want to become professional composers, performers or teachers of music.

Royal College of Nursing, the (RCN) (medicine)
See **Nurses**.

Royal commission (government)
An occasional state body, first developed in the nineteenth century, consisting of eminent independent individuals appointed by the government to inquire into a specific area and recommend changes or proposals. The government is under no obligation to follow its recommendations.

Royal Court Theatre, the (arts)
See **English Stage Company**.

Royal family, the (royalty)
The British royal family consists of the sovereign and his or her closest family, collectively known as the House of Windsor. The current inner family comprises Queen Elizabeth, the Duke of Edinburgh, Queen Elizabeth the Queen Mother, the Prince and Princess of Wales, the Queen's other three children and the Queen's sister, Princess Margaret. The extended royal family also includes the Queen's cousins, the Dukes of Gloucester and Kent, and the

spouses and children of these and other relations. The royal dukes are also princes because of their membership of the royal family and there are currently five: the Duke of Edinburgh, the Duke of Cornwall, the Duke of York, the Duke of Gloucester and the Duke of Kent.

Royal Festival Hall, the (RFH) (arts)
A leading concert hall, constructed between 1948 and 1951, which is part of a complex of cultural buildings on the South Bank of the Thames, London, and which is a forum for performances of mainly classical music.

Royal Greenwich Observatory, the (science)
Britain's main astronomical observatory originally established at Greenwich, London, in 1675. It has been moved several times since, to Sussex and then to Cambridge University, with some of its telescopes now in the Canary Islands. The observatory has historically been in charge of accurate time measurement in Britain, and for the world time-zones which are based on Greenwich Mean Time (GMT).

Royal International Agricultural Show, the (agriculture)
An influential international agricultural exhibition held annually over four days in July at Stoneleigh, Warwickshire, at which the latest products of British agriculture (produce, animals and machinery) are on display. Other important agricultural shows are the Bath and West in Somerset and the Royal Smithfield Show in London.

Royal International Horse Show, the (sport and leisure)
A show-jumping competition for international and British riders which takes place annually at the National Exhibition Centre (NEC), Birmingham.

Royal Mail, the (RM) (communications)
The ancient and official title for that section of the state Post Office (PO) which is responsible for the collection, transportation and delivery of letters and parcels.

Royal Marines, the (RM) (military)
A body of sea-going soldiers, originally created in 1664, and today forming part of the Royal Navy. The Marines, including their specialist Commando groups, engage in attacks on enemy coasts from ships and prepare the way for other forces.

Royal Military Academy, the (RMA) (military)
A professional and educational college originally established in 1799 which trains cadets to become officers in the British Army, now at Sandhurst, Berkshire and commonly known as Sandhurst.

Royal Mint, the (finance)
The government department that produces metal currency coins for circulation in Britain, established in 1811, and now based near Cardiff, Wales.

Royal Navy, the (RN) (military)
The British navy, officially created as an organized body in the sixteenth century, is Britain's oldest armed force and is known as the Senior Service. It is now the smallest military wing with some 62,000 men and women, including the Royal Marines, and operates the submarines of the independent nuclear deterrent. The Fleet Air Arm is the aviation branch of the navy, operating both from shore bases and from aircraft carriers.

Royal Opera, the (arts)
An opera company, established in 1946, which is based at the Royal Opera House, Covent Garden, London. It performs a classical and modern opera programme, and tours in Britain and worldwide.

Royal Philharmonic Orchestra, the (RPO) (arts)
A well known symphony orchestra, established in 1946, and based in London. It performs mainly classical music under a series of leading conductors.

Royal salute (royalty)
The annual firing of guns or cannon in central London (at such places as the Tower of London and Hyde Park) to commemorate, among other occasions, the opening of Parliament, royal births, and the accession and coronation of the sovereign.

Royal Shakespeare Company, the (RSC) (arts)
A leading (and the second most prolific after the National Theatre) theatre company originally established in 1879 with the opening of the Shakespeare Memorial Theatre in Stratford-upon-Avon, Warwickshire. It now operates both from this theatre and the Barbican Theatre in London, and performs Shakespearean and other plays.

Royal Smithfield Show (agriculture)
See **Royal International Agricultural Show**.

Royal Society, the (RS) (science)
The oldest and most prestigious scientific society in Britain, established in 1645 in London to promote discussion of scientific discoveries and having prominent scientists among its members. It is also concerned with science education, elects leading academics as Fellows, arranges international exchanges and conferences, and advises the government on scientific policy.

Royal Society of Arts, the (RSA) (education)
An educational and learned society established in 1754 to promote the arts, commerce and manufacturing. Today it provides lecture programmes and organizes examinations in languages and commercial subjects in Britain and overseas.

Royal standard, the (royalty)
The personal flag of the sovereign which is flown from buildings, such as Buckingham Palace, to indicate that he or she is in residence. It carries the monarch's insignia or arms and is older than any other national flag in Britain.

Royal Tournament, the (sport and leisure)
An annual military exhibition at Earls Court in London, at which members of the armed forces give displays such as motor-cycle acrobatics, the dismantling and reassembling of field guns, dog-handling exercises and massed band marches.

Royal Ulster Constabulary, the (RUC) (law)
The police force in Northern Ireland, consisting of full- and part-time members, established in 1922, and which is responsible for maintaining law and order in the province (often in co-operation with the British Army).

Royal Variety Show, the (arts)
An annual light entertainment and social occasion attended by the royal family, which is performed by well known variety artists in aid of charity (such as the Variety Artists' Federation).

Rugby Football (sport and leisure)
A type of football which is different from Association Football (soccer), played with an oval (rather than a round) ball, which may be handled in addition to being kicked. It was formally established in 1871 when the Football Association prohibited the handling of the ball in football (soccer) matches. See **Rugby League (RL)** and **Rugby Union (RU)**.

Rugby League (RL) (sport and leisure)
One of the two codes of Rugby Football, which has teams of 13 players instead of 15 (as in Rugby Union), and is now largely a professional game, although amateurs do play at the lower levels. The sport was established in 1893 because professional players were banned from Rugby Union, is mostly identified with the north of England which has the top clubs, and has somewhat different rules from Rugby Union.

Rugby Union (RU) (sport and leisure)
One of the two codes of Rugby Football (commonly known as rugger), which has teams of 15 players instead of 13 (as in Rugby League). It is a strictly amateur sport, originating in the type of football played at Rugby School (a leading public school) in the early 1800s, with somewhat different rules from Rugby League.

Rule of law (government)
The principle that all government agents and law enforcers shall operate according to and within the law, and adhere to ideas of fairness and natural justice. It implies limits on legislative and executive power and equal access to and equality before the law. The value of the principle has been questioned, but it is still important in helping to restrain the arbitrary power of government.

Runnymede (government)
The place on the south bank of the Thames in Surrey where King John was forced by Anglo-Norman barons to sign the Magna Carta in June 1215. The charter is traditionally regarded as the first constitutional document to state the civil liberties of citizens (albeit the nobility historically) against the arbitrary power of the monarch.

S

Safe seat (government)
A parliamentary constituency whose sitting MP is regularly elected
to the House of Commons by a large and comfortable majority
of the popular vote. These safe seats, such as Conservative-held
constituencies in southern England and Labour-held constituencies
in northern England, Scotland and South Wales, form the large
majority in the British electoral system and very rarely change their
voting patterns.

Safety net (society)
A term to describe the basic facilities and financial resources which
are available to the neediest of citizens under the social security
and national health systems in Britain.

Sainsbury's (commerce)
A store, established in 1869 in London, which has developed into
a major private company with quality supermarkets selling a range
of food and other products in most towns and cities throughout the
country and is Britain's biggest food group. Similar stores are Tesco
throughout the country and Waitrose in southern England.

Salary (employment and finance)
The amount of money which is earned by an individual (such as
professionals and higher income earners) in employment, and which
is normally paid monthly. It is usually distinguished from wages.

Salvation Army, the (SA) (religion)
A uniformed Christian (Protestant non-Anglican) organization
(commonly known as Sally's Army), founded by William Booth in
London in 1865, which engages in evangelical and welfare work
worldwide. It is motivated by a practical social concern, dedicated
to giving aid and spiritual comfort to the underprivileged, and is a
familiar sight on British streets with its public services, hymn singing
and bands.

Sandhurst (military)
See **Royal Military Academy**.

Sandwich course (education)
A specially constructed educational programme by which students are able to combine a full-time study course at an institution of further or higher education with periods of work experience in a factory, office or company.

Satellite television (media)
A system of broadcasting television over a very wide distance by means of an orbiting space satellite, and which is received through a satellite dish placed outside a home. Satellite television was introduced into Britain in 1989 and is now supplied by the British Sky Broadcasting (B-Sky-B) company from the Astra and Marcopolo satellites.

Scholarship (education)
A financial grant awarded by an independent school to a pupil who has passed an entrance examination to the school with high marks. The scholarship will usually pay for the pupil's fees, books, uniform and any boarding costs.

School Examination and Assessment Council, the (SEAC) (education)
The body which approves all examination, syllabus and assessment content and procedures in state schools in England and Wales.

School fees (education)
The money which is paid by a parent (or a scholarship) for a child's education at an independent (private) school in Britain.

School governors (education)
Individuals who, on an unpaid and part-time basis, help with the organization of a school in Britain, in both the state and independent sectors of education. Recent Conservative government reforms in state schools have increased the duties and powers of governors. Governors may be divided into appointed (school governors) and elected (parent governors) positions.

School inspectors (education)
Civil servants (known officially as Her Majesty's Inspectors of Schools [HMIs]) and local authority advisers who previously had the job of inspecting and preparing reports on state and independent schools in Britain. The service has now been privatized to operate from 1993 as a self-governing inspections agency to be known as the Office for Standards in Education (Ofsted).

School welfare officer (education)
A social worker (usually employed by the local government social services) who is responsible for the social, personal and educational welfare of state schoolchildren in a particular area.

Science park (education and science)
A recent development in Britain where a separate area of an institution of higher education is set aside for use by private companies to carry out research and exhibit their latest technology. There are currently some 30 science parks in Britain.

Scotland (geography)
The most northerly country of the United Kingdom, with a population of 5.1 million, and with England to its south. Scotland is a largely mountainous area with characteristic lochs (lakes) and fiord coastlines, and has long had independent legal, banking and educational systems. Scottish languages, such as Gaelic and Scots, are still spoken by some Scottish people, and there have been recent increased calls for independence (or devolution) for Scotland from the UK.

Scottish Certificate of Education, the (SCE) (education)
The national school-leaving Scottish examination at secondary level which is the counterpart to the GCSE and A-levels in England and Wales, with a Standard grade examination at the end of the fourth year and the Higher grade examination at the end of the fifth or sixth year.

Scottish Examination Board, the (education)
The national body which reviews and controls all aspects of school examinations and assessment in Scotland.

Scottish National Party, the (SNP) (politics)
The leading nationalist political party in Scotland, established in 1928, which campaigns for the independence of Scotland from the United Kingdom. The party has had varied success in attracting local and national support for its programme of a separate, culturally distinctive and economically independent Scotland. It did not do as well as expected in the 1992 general election and has three MPs in the House of Commons.

Scout Association, the (sport and leisure)
An international youth organization (with Cub Scouts from 11–16 and Venture Scouts from 16–20) headed by a Chief Scout and founded in 1908 by Lord Baden-Powell to train boys to develop

their initiative, practical skills and sense of responsibility. Girls can now (1992) become members.

Sealink UK Ltd (transport)
A private company that provides extensive ship and hovercraft (through the Hoverspeed company) ferry services from mainland Britain to the Continent, the Isle of Wight, the Channel Islands, the Isle of Man and Ireland.

Season ticket (transport and arts)
A ticket, usually purchased in advance and for a specific period of time (such as a week, month or year), which permits the holder to have regular travel facilities on public transport, or which allows admission to concerts, theatres, films, exhibitions and a range of sporting events (such as football matches).

Seat (government)
The common name for a parliamentary constituency in the sense that victory in a constituency election enables an MP to have a seat in the House of Commons.

Second class (communications and education)
1. The cheaper of the two Post Office postal rates for letters (the other being first class) which results in a slower delivery. 2. The class of an honours degree which is the one obtained by most students in institutions of higher education. It is usually divided into two sections (2i and 2ii) with the first denoting higher merit.

Second reading (government)
The second stage in the passage of a bill through Parliament (whether presented in the House of Commons or House of Lords), which usually involves a debate on the principles of the bill.

Secondary modern school (education)
A state secondary school in England and Wales historically deriving from the 1944 Education Act, intended for children who had failed the 11-plus examination and entry to a grammar school, and which provided a generally non-academic education. The system has now been largely replaced by comprehensive schools and only a small minority of secondary level children attend such schools.

Secondary school (education)
British secondary education caters for schoolchildren between the ages of 11(12) and 18, and is provided by secondary schools in both the state and independent sectors, with the majority of pupils leav-

ing at 16. Most state schools are comprehensives, to which some 90 per cent of children in this age group go, but there are still some remaining grammar schools, secondary modern schools and technical schools (2.5 per cent of children). The independent sector has a variety of schools, with most providing secondary education from 11 to 18 (public schools from 13) for some 7.5 per cent of the age group.

Secretary of state (government)
A senior minister of the Crown who is head of one of the major government departments, such as the Home Office, Foreign Office, Trade and Industry, the Environment, Education and Health.

Securities and Investment Board, the (SIB) (finance)
An independent government-appointed board which supervises the activities, organization and conduct of those investment businesses and City (of London) financial institutions which operate under the Financial Services Act 1986 and give advice on financial investments to the public.

Security of tenure (housing and law)
A tenant renting property in the private and public sectors of housing cannot be removed from the property (except in the case of special short tenancies) without very good reason, and in effect has a right to stay permanently.

Select committee (law and government)
A committee appointed by either House of Parliament to review or investigate some matter of public interest. Most select committees are House of Commons bodies which oversee the workings and expenditure of specific departments, or examine government policies in a range of areas.

Self-governing (NHS) trusts (medicine)
Conservative government reforms in the National Health Service since 1990 have allowed some NHS hospitals to become self-governing trusts. This means that they are responsible for running their own affairs and deciding their priorities, are independent of local health authority control, are funded directly by central government through general taxation, and are accountable to the Department of Health. They are still state hospitals within the NHS.

Self-regulation (finance)
The internal arrangements by which organizations such as newspapers and the financial institutions of the City (of London) regulate

themselves as to their conduct and codes of practice, outside state or government supervision.

Semester (education)
See **Academic (school) year** and **Term**.

Semi-detached house (housing)
A house which is joined on one of its walls to another house of similar design. Such properties are usually cheaper than fully detached houses.

Senior citizen (society)
See **Old age pensioner**.

Sergeant-at-Arms (government)
The officer of the House of Commons who is appointed by the Crown to serve the Speaker and who is responsible for maintaining order in, and the internal administration of, the House. He enforces the orders of the Speaker and the House.

Serious Fraud Office, the (SFO) (government and finance)
The government department which is responsible for investigating and prosecuting serious and complex fraud cases under the supervision of the Attorney-General in England, Wales and Northern Ireland (the Crown Office Fraud Unit in Scotland). It has a staff of police, lawyers, accountants and other specialists. In London it co-operates with the Fraud Squad, a specialist police branch of the Metropolitan Police and the City of London Police.

Service areas (transport)
Sections of a motorway at regular intervals where petrol service stations and rest facilities for drivers and travellers are available.

Service charge (commerce)
A sum of money normally amounting to some 10 per cent of the total charge for a restaurant meal that represents a commission for service and which is added to the bill. Most restaurant meals today include a service charge, but if there is none then the customer can choose how much to give (a tip), if anything, for the service.

Service sector (finance)
That sector of the national economy which provides services, rather than manufactured products, such as leisure activities and financial advice on investments. This sector increased dramatically in the 1980s, but has suffered in the recession of the late 1980s and early 1990s.

Service station (transport)
A private garage, often placed prominently on a busy road, that sells petrol, oil and other motoring products, and also repairs, services and tests vehicles.

Session (government)
The full five-year duration of a Parliament is divided up into sessions, with each session usually lasting for about one year, normally beginning in October or November, with provisions for the recall of Parliament during the summer and other breaks.

Set book (education)
A book which is compulsory reading for pupils and students in a school or institution of further and higher education, and which usually forms the basis for examinations or project work.

Settlement out of court (law)
In civil law cases, which can be very expensive and time-consuming if taken to a full court trial, the arrangement whereby the parties agree between themselves to settle the case out of court, that is, before it comes to trial.

Sex Discrimination Act (government)
See **Equal Opportunities Commission**.

Shadow Cabinet, the (government)
When the Labour Party is the opposition party in the House of Commons its Shadow Cabinet mainly consists of a small group of Labour MPs who are elected by the party MPs to shadow or oversee the work of a government minister and his or her department, becoming, for example, the Shadow Minister for the Environment. Should the Opposition win the next general election, these shadow ministers will normally become government ministers. When the Conservative Party is in opposition, its Shadow Cabinet is chosen by the Leader of the Party.

Shadow ministers (government)
Those MPs of the opposition party in the House of Commons (currently the Labour Party) who form the Shadow Cabinet and who shadow or specialize in the same area as a government minister, such as the Home Secretary or Secretary of State for Education.

Shaftesbury Avenue (London and arts)
A street in central London near Piccadilly Circus which has been traditionally regarded as London's entertainment centre and is well known for its large number of theatres and cinemas.

Shakespeare Memorial Theatre (arts)
The original theatre in Stratford-upon-Avon, Warwickshire, was built in 1879 and performed Shakespearean plays. It was destroyed by fire in 1926 and replaced by the present theatre (now formally called the Royal Shakespeare Theatre), which provides an annual season of Shakespeare's plays by the Royal Shakespeare Company, usually prior to their performance at the Barbican Theatre in London.

Shareholder (finance)
A person who has bought and therefore holds shares in a commercial company. Shareholders are legally the owners of such companies and will receive dividends on any trading profits.

Sheltered housing (society)
Usually small flats or rooms in specially constructed properties which provide safe and secure housing and services for elderly and retired people. The property will usually have modern communications equipment and a resident warden who is in charge. Sheltered housing may be provided by local government authorities or private commercial companies.

Sheriff (law)
A judicial official in Scotland who decides cases in the sheriff courts which handle both civil and criminal cases.

Shop steward (employment)
The influential official of a trade union branch in a place of work such as a factory, company, office or local government council. He or she will be involved in negotiations about wages and conditions of employment with employers and may initiate strike action.

Sickness benefit (finance)
A state benefit (currently £41.20 per week for up to 28 weeks) within the social security system which is paid to self-employed people and employees when they are sick for at least four days and do not qualify for statutory sick pay from their employers.

Single European Market (Act), the (SEM/SEA) (government)
The Single European Act 1986 (SEA) specified that economic integration among the member-states of the European Community (EC) should be completed by the end of 1992, so that there would be a free movement of labour (people), services, trade and capital throughout a single EC market (SEM).

Sinn Fein (politics)
The Irish nationalist or republican political party (meaning 'ourselves'), founded in 1905, which earlier campaigned for the complete separation of Ireland from Britain and which now, as the political wing of the Provisional IRA, fights for Northern Ireland to be united with the Republic of Ireland. It has achieved some success in local and UK elections in Northern Ireland, but lost its one House of Commons representative in the 1992 general election.

Sit-in (politics and employment)
A civil or employment protest or demonstration in response to a grievance in which protesters sit down in or occupy premises belonging to those against whom the protest is delivered, such as council workers in a council meeting chamber or students in a vice-chancellor's office.

Sitting tenant (housing)
A person who occupies rented accommodation, whether public or private, and who pays rent to a landlord. He or she usually has security of tenure and cannot easily be removed.

Sixth form (education)
The senior class in a secondary school in England and Wales, whether state or independent, in which 16–18-year-old pupils are studying for A-level examinations. It is normally divided into a lower sixth form and an upper sixth form according to age.

Sixth form college (education)
Normally a special further education college provided currently by a local government authority for students from the age of 16 (including mature students) who wish to take a wide range of courses and examinations, such as the GCSE and A-levels.

Sleeping partner (finance)
A partner in a business venture (such as a partnership) who does not participate actively in the running of the concern. He or she will normally have contributed capital (money) to the venture and expects to take a share of any profits.

Slums (housing)
Usually areas of big cities where the housing stock is in very bad condition and barely fit for human habitation. Most of the worst British slums were cleared by the 1960s, but areas of decay and deprivation still exist.

Smith's (WH) (commerce)
A well known company that runs shops and stores throughout Britain, and which specializes in selling newspapers, books, magazines, office equipment, stationery, records and cassettes. A well known competitor is the John Menzies chain of stores.

Social and Liberal Democratic Party, the (SLD) (politics)
A left-of-centre political party formed in 1987–8 by the merger of the Social Democratic Party and the Liberal Party. The SLD, which is the third largest political party in Britain, sees itself as a credible alternative to the Conservative Party and the Labour Party. Known as the SLD or Democrats, but the Liberal Democrats has been its official short name since 1988.

Social Democratic and Labour Party, the (SDLP) (politics)
A political party formed in Northern Ireland in 1970 by moderate Catholics who rejected the use of violence in the province. It works for closer political links between Northern Ireland and the Republic of Ireland, and has unification of the north and south as a long-term aim.

Social Fund, the (finance)
A form of benefit in the social security system. Certain discretionary payments (formerly known as one-payment benefits) may be made by Social Security offices in the form of loans or grants to people on low incomes to allow them to cope with a crisis or exceptional situation, but they have become increasingly difficult to obtain.

Social security (finance)
State financial benefits or help (such as income support) which are paid to people who are in need and who may not have contributed to the national insurance scheme, and benefits (such as sickness, unemployment and pension payments) for those who have contributed. The money spent on social security amounts to almost one-third of government spending and is raised from public taxation and the national insurance scheme.

Social Services, the (society and government)
That area of the British social welfare system which provides personal services for elderly and disabled people and their carers, children and young people, and families. Much of this work is carried out by professionals and currently provided by local government social services departments.

Social workers (society and government)
Professionally trained and qualified individuals who are employed
by local authorities, the National Health Service (NHS) and voluntary organizations to provide a network of special care services in
the community for those in need, such as children, the elderly, the
handicapped, the sick and the disadvantaged.

Solicitor (law)
One of the two types of qualified lawyer (with barristers) in England
and Wales who advises clients on a range of legal matters, such as
conveyancing, crime, business, divorce and probate, and who can
appear for the client in the magistrates' court and the county court
(where they are often known as solicitor-advocates). He or she is
normally a member of the Law Society, the solicitors' professional
association.

Solicitor-General, the (SG) (law)
The state law officer of the Crown in England and Wales who ranks
second to the Attorney-General in the government legal hierarchy
and who performs any duties that the Attorney-General may delegate. There is a similar position in Scotland.

Solicitors' Complaints Bureau, the (law)
An independent body, separate from the Law Society, which hears
and rules on complaints by dissatisfied clients against solicitors.

Sotheby's (commerce)
A leading firm of auctioneers in London, established in 1744 and
reputedly the largest in the world. It holds auctions of a wide range
of objects for which world record prices are achieved, but tends to
specialize in fine art, rare books and manuscripts.

South Bank, the (London and arts)
The name associated with a group of cultural buildings on the south
bank of the River Thames in central London near Waterloo Bridge.
The site contains concert halls, theatres and galleries such as the
Royal Festival Hall, the Queen Elizabeth Hall, the National Thea-
tre, the National Film Theatre and the Hayward Gallery.

Sovereign (royalty)
Another term for the British monarch (queen or king), which indicates the former power or sovereignty of the monarch.

Sovereignty (government)
A term to describe the authority which Britain as a state has both

internally in the country, and externally in its relations with other nations. It is often tied to the legal or legislative sovereignty of Parliament, but today in practice rests with the sitting government for its implementation.

Speaker, the (government)
The chief official of the House of Commons, who is an elected MP and chosen by his or her fellow MPs to chair all debates and proceedings and to keep order in the Chamber. As a servant and agent of the House he or she has to apply its rules and traditions impartially and with regard to the rights and privileges of members.

Speakers' Corner, the (London)
The north-east corner of Hyde Park, London, which has traditionally been the place for people to congregate for open-air speaking and debate, covering a variety of opinions and beliefs. It has been popularly seen as an example of the right of free speech, and used as such since 1872 when the right of assembly was legally recognized.

Special Air Service, the (SAS) (military)
A special force (or regiment) of the British Army established originally in 1942. It comprises trained and specialist troops who undertake secret operations in war and peace.

Special Branch, the (SB) (law)
The specialist section of a regional police force that operates primarily in the areas of political security and intelligence-gathering in Britain, but also has national protection duties for public figures.

Special constable (law)
A volunteer, male or female, who provides part-time and unpaid police duties under the supervision of the regular police in his or her local area.

Special school (education)
A school, whether state or private, which specializes in the needs of children from 2 to 19 who suffer from physical or mental handicaps and who are unable to benefit from ordinary schools, although there have been recent attempts at greater integration of such children into standard schools.

Speech day (education)
An annual event in many British schools for teachers, pupils and parents, at which school prizes are presented, reports are delivered

by the headteacher and senior pupils, and a speech is made by a visiting speaker.

Speech from the Throne, the (government and royalty)
See **Opening (State), (of Parliament)**.

Sports Council, the (sport and leisure)
An independent organization established in 1972, with national councils in England, Scotland and Wales, which encourages sports participation and increased sports facilities, and co-operates with local authorities and voluntary bodies.

Squash (rackets) (sport and leisure)
Usually a game for two or four players in an enclosed indoor court, reputedly originating at Harrow School (a leading public school) in the early nineteenth century. A small rubber ball is struck off any wall of the court with a racket, but must land on the front wall above a painted line to score. It has evolved into a very popular amateur and professional sport.

St Andrew's Day (society)
On 30 November is the religious festival of St Andrew (Scotland's patron saint), traditionally seen as Scotland's national day and an occasion for wearing a thistle (the national emblem).

St David's Day (society)
On 1 March is the religious festival of St David (the patron saint of Wales), traditionally seen as Wales's national day and an occasion for wearing a daffodil or leek (the national emblems).

St George's Day (society)
On 23 April is the religious festival of St George (England's patron saint), traditionally seen as England's national day and an occasion for some people to wear a rose (the national emblem).

St John Ambulance (Brigade), the (medicine)
A well known voluntary body, established in 1877, whose unpaid and part-time volunteers supply first aid at public events and on sporting occasions. It also supplies nursing services in hospitals and residential homes.

St Patrick's Day (society)
On 17 March is the religious festival of St Patrick (Ireland's patron saint), traditionally seen as Northern Ireland's (and the Republic's) national day, and a bank holiday.

St Paul's (Cathedral) (London and religion)
There has been a religious building on this site in East London
since medieval times, but the earlier ones have been destroyed.
The present cathedral was designed by Sir Christopher Wren
(1632–1723), is one of London's best known buildings, a centre for
national religious occasions, and contains the tombs and monuments
of distinguished people in British history.

Staff (employment)
A term for the personnel or employees of a company or business,
and also the teachers in a school.

Staff association (employment)
A professional body similar to a trade union which represents the
interests of its members, such as the Police Federation and the
British Medical Association.

Stamp duty (finance)
A state tax which is levied on the conveyance or sale of property,
such as a house. Over a certain value the tax charged is 1 per cent
per £1,000.

Stand for Parliament (politics)
The decision of an individual, usually before being adopted as a
prospective candidate by a local constituency party, to attempt
election to the House of Commons. The term can also be used
after adoption.

Standing committees (government)
Committees of the House of Commons, chosen proportionally to
the parties' strengths in the House, which give detailed consider-
ation to public parliamentary bills during their passage through the
House. The standing committee system may also be used in other
areas of British life.

Standing orders (finance)
Written notification from customers to their banks stipulating that
regular and specific amounts of money from their accounts should
be transferred to the accounts of named persons or bodies.

Stansted (Airport) (transport)
Britain's third biggest international airport near Stansted, Essex,
which handles scheduled, charter and cargo traffic.

State (the) (society)
A term to describe all the bodies which collectively have legal

authority in Britain, such as the government, the monarch, and central and local government, and which carry out their activities in the name of the state.

State education (education)
A term used to differentiate non-fee-paying education provided by the state from private fee-paying education supplied by the independent sector.

State schools (education)
Non-fee-paying primary and secondary schools which are mostly controlled and financed by the state through a local education authority (LEA) of the county or regional council, and in England and Wales may be either county or voluntary schools. The vast majority of schools in Britain are state schools (some 93 per cent as opposed to some 7 per cent in the independent sector).

Statute (government and law)
A bill which has passed through all stages of Parliament and has become an Act of Parliament or a statute. Such an Act is placed on the Statute Book as representing the law of the land, and the body of such law is known as statute law.

Statutory sick pay (SSP) (finance and employment)
The statutory payment (currently either £45.30 or £52.50 per week depending on average weekly wages) made by an employer to an employee when the latter is absent from work because of sickness for up to a maximum of 28 weeks. People who cannot claim the full SSP can be paid the state sickness benefit, and those entitled neither to SSP nor sickness benefit can claim the state invalidity benefit.

Stipendiary magistrate (law)
A legally qualified professional lawyer (barrister or solicitor) who sits alone as a judge in some magistrates' courts in the large cities of England and Wales to decide mainly criminal cases. He or she is a professional element in an otherwise amateur magistrates' system of summary law.

Stock Exchange, the (SE) (finance)
The independent institution in the City (of London), together with other exchanges throughout Britain, established in 1802, which is a financial market for the buying and selling of stocks and shares at market prices and where industry and companies may raise capital from investors.

Stockbroker (finance)
Traditionally a member of the Stock Exchange in London (sometimes still known as a broker) who acted as a buyer and seller of stocks and shares for investors through a jobber (who actually set the prices). There is no longer a distinction between jobbers and brokers, and stocks and shares may now be bought and sold directly through a broker or dealer.

Stock(s) (finance)
The financial capital of a corporation or company which is contributed by individuals to the business and which is divided into shares entitling the holders of the shares to a proportion of the business profits.

Stonehenge (geography)
See **English Heritage**.

Stormont (government)
The large building commonly known as Stormont but officially as Parliament House outside Belfast, Northern Ireland, built in 1932, which contained the Northern Ireland parliament from partition in 1921 until direct rule in 1972, and which now serves mainly as a British government administrative centre for Northern Ireland.

Strangers' Gallery, the (government)
The upper galleries or rows of seats in the House of Commons and House of Lords where the general public is allowed to sit and listen to debates and proceedings in the two Houses.

Streaming (education)
The traditional practice in state secondary schools, which still exists in the comprehensive system, of dividing pupils into separate sections of a class according to either their ability or the different subjects that they may be studying.

Strict liability (law)
A legal term to describe the absolute responsibility which a manufacturer has in law to the purchaser or consumer of his or her products if these are faulty and cause damage to property or persons. This concept is important in consumer sales.

Strike (employment)
A withdrawal of labour by employees in a place of work or nationally in order to further an industrial dispute. British strikes must be called by the executive committee of a trade union and

approved by a written ballot of all union members to have legal effect. A striker is an individual who is engaged in such an industrial dispute, and he or she may be given strike pay by a trade union during a strike to compensate for lost wages.

Student (education)
An individual studying an educational programme in further and higher education, rather than at school level (where schoolchildren are traditionally called pupils).

Student grant, the (education)
Any qualified British student who has obtained a place at an institution of higher education in Britain is entitled to receive a grant of money from his or her local education authority (LEA) which pays for tuition fees and the maintenance of the student during term time. The maintenance part of the grant is dependent upon a means test of parents' income. In 1990 the grant was frozen at the then levels by the Conservative government, requiring students to take out a 'top up' loan (to be repaid with interest) from a government-sponsored body if they needed further money for maintenance.

Sub judice (law)
The legal rule which stipulates that the media and individuals must not make any comments on a court case which is proceeding, except to describe the facts of those proceedings. Any person or organization infringing the rule may be punished by the judge for contempt of court (a fine or imprisonment).

Subscriber (finance)
An individual who pays a sum of money (or subscription) in order to become a member of an organization supplying a service, such as a satellite television company, a book or sports club, or a magazine.

Subscriber trunk dialling (STD) (communications)
The method by which a telephone caller can communicate directly with another person in Britain or overseas without having to be connected by a central operator or switchboard.

Sub-titles (media)
The text in English which appears at the bottom of a television or cinema screen in Britain when a foreign-language film or programme is being shown.

Suburbia (housing)
A residential area (the suburbs) which lies outside the central

districts of a town or city, and which may be equated with a higher social position.

Suffragan bishop (religion)
A junior or assistant bishop, usually in the Church of England and the Roman Catholic Church, who is responsible for the organization of a smaller district within the larger diocese.

Suffrage (government and politics)
The possession of the right to vote in British elections held by most adult people resident in Britain and some Britons overseas.

Summary offence (law)
A criminal offence of a less serious nature than an indictable offence, which is triable only in a magistrates' court without a jury.

Summoning of Parliament (government)
The writ which the monarch, on the advice of the Prime Minister, issues to call a new Parliament to Westminster for the start of a new term or session.

Summons (law)
An official legal order, frequently delivered by post or sometimes personally by a court bailiff, to an individual requiring his or her attendance at a court of law, to answer a criminal charge or to give evidence in a court case.

Sunday school (religion)
The voluntary educational classes that are organized by many different Christian churches and chapels in their religious buildings on Sundays, and which provide children with religious teaching and basic Christian instruction. The lessons may be given either by the priest or minister, or by a lay member of the church or chapel.

Supply teacher (education)
A temporary schoolteacher who replaces (or substitutes for) a permanent teacher, who may be away sick, in a school for a period of time. Supply teachers are usually on a register compiled by the local education authority (LEA) which 'supplies' them to local schools.

Supreme Court (of Judicature), the (law)
A collective court in England and Wales established in 1873 by the amalgamation of many ancient courts into one administrative and judicial unit, today comprising the Court of Appeal, the High Court

of Justice and the crown courts. The Supreme Court has its headquarters in the Royal Courts of Justice in the Strand, London.

Surgery (medicine)
The common name for a general practitioner's (GP's) office, where
patients will meet their doctor. This may be in a group practice
clinic or health centre, or in the premises of a sole practitioner.

Suspended sentence (law)
A court sentence on a convicted criminal may be suspended (be
inoperative) for a given period, provided the person does not re-
offend within that time. Usually given to people who are guilty of
relatively minor crimes, or for whom there are special extenuating
circumstances.

Swearing in (law)
The ceremony often used when an official legally takes over a new
job or position, such as a judge, new peer or new Member of
Parliament (MP), during which he or she promises to uphold the
duties of the position.

Synod, (General), the (religion)
The central governing body of the Church of England, which meets
at least twice a year. It deals with such church matters as education,
inter-church relations, recruitment of clergy, and questions of
worship and religious practice. Church House in London is the
headquarters of the Synod. Local affairs in the individual dioceses
are governed by a diocesan synod.

T

Tabloid (media)
The common name for newspapers with small-size pages (as opposed to broadsheet, or large-page, papers) which usually means the national popular press.

Take-home pay (employment)
The net amount of money that an employee takes home (or has left) after all deductions, such as income tax and national insurance contributions, have been removed from his or her gross or total wage or salary.

Takeover (commerce)
The procedure when one company (usually a powerful or dominant one) takes control and ownership of another company (usually a smaller and loss-making one), in order to increase its share of the particular market.

Tate (Gallery), the (TG) (arts)
A well known art gallery in London, established in 1897, which contains an extensive collection of British and foreign paintings, and modern sculpture. It also serves as an art education centre and holds prestigious exhibitions, not only of paintings but also other artistic artefacts.

Tax disc (transport)
The official round paper document purchased by a vehicle's owner (often from a post office) that is attached to the inner, lower lefthand corner of the vehicle's windscreen to indicate that it has been formally licensed by the Department of Transport for use on the road for a specific period of time.

Tax relief (finance)
An amount of money which is treated as a deduction from total tax. For example, an individual in Britain can obtain tax relief on a loan or mortgage up to £30,000 which is taken out to buy a house or flat.

Tax system, the (finance)
The British tax system consists of levies or charges by the state,

which have to be passed annually by Parliament, on income arising from two main sources: direct taxes on incomes, profits and wealth, and indirect taxes on goods and services.

Taxable income (finance)
The net amount of money or income on which an individual or company must pay income tax in Britain, after all allowances and permitted deductions from the gross sum have been made.

Tax-exempt (finance)
An amount of money, also known as tax-free, which is not subject to income tax in Britain, such as interest from certain government savings bonds.

Teaching hospital (medicine)
A large general hospital, usually in a university city, where medical students pursue the clinical part of their degree course as they train to become doctors and nurses. Well known teaching hospitals in London are St Bartholomew's, Middlesex and Guy's Hospitals.

Technical college (education)
A college of further education (previously under the control of a local government education authority but now self-governing and commonly known as a 'tech') which offers sub-degree educational programmes in a wide range of technical, secretarial, art and semi-professional subjects.

Technical school (education)
The old educational system from 1944 created state secondary schools (known as technical schools) which offered an alternative educational programme that combined academic and technical courses for suitable pupils. There is only a very small number of such schools remaining in some parts of England and Wales, attended by a small minority of secondary level pupils.

Telecom (British) Tower, the (London and communications)
A dominant feature of the London skyline, the 580-feet (176-m) high Telecom Tower was constructed in 1965 as a transmitting and receiving centre for radio, television and telephone services.

Teletext (media)
Written information on a range of subjects (such as the latest weather and news) which appears on the screen of a television set adapted for this service, after the owner has purchased the relevant receiver. The ITC offers Oracle, the BBC provides Ceefax and British Telecom organizes Prestel.

Television licence (media)
The licence that must be paid for by every householder possessing one or more television sets. The current annual cost of a television licence is £80 for a colour set (the majority) and £22.50 for a black and white set, and is set by Parliament. The licence fee finances the operations of the BBC (but not the ITC).

Temporary accommodation (housing and government)
The housing, usually in a hotel or bed-and-breakfast establishment, which a local authority is obliged to provide for homeless individuals and families in its area while they wait for a more permanent residence.

Tenant (housing and commerce)
An individual who pays rent to a landlord or landlady for the use of living accommodation, such as a house or flat, or to a landlord for business premises, such as an office.

Tender (finance)
A financial offer which a private company makes for the purchase of property, shares or a service. The term is used, for example, when local government services, such as laundry and catering in a National Health Service hospital, are offered by competitive tendering to companies in the private sector, rather than the hospital itself providing the service.

Term (education)
Normally the three periods into which the academic year of an educational institution is divided. Generally they are the autumn term from September to December, the winter term from January to March, and the summer term from April to July. Some institutions of higher education are moving to a semester system, which strictly is a six-month period.

Terraced houses (housing)
A row of small houses, each (except for the end ones) connected on both sides to the neighbouring houses, which forms a continuous line in a street. They may be old properties in a town or city, but some contemporary developments are also built in this style.

Territorial Army, the (TA) (military)
A volunteer military reserve force of some 80,000 trained men and women whose role is to supplement regular troops in times of national emergency. It keeps in readiness by holding training exercises with the permanent armed forces.

Tertiary education (education)
State tertiary (third level) education in England and Wales (also known as further education) is taken after primary and secondary education. Tertiary colleges, such as sixth-form colleges and colleges of further education, offer a range of part- and full-time academic, non-academic and vocational courses for students over 16.

Test match (sport and leisure)
An international cricket match over five days in the summer in England, played on a cricket ground such as Lord's or the Oval in London, Trent Bridge in Nottingham, Edgbaston in Birmingham or Old Trafford in Manchester, between the England cricket team and teams from Commonwealth countries such as Australia, New Zealand, India, Sri Lanka, Pakistan and the West Indies, which usually forms one of five test matches in a competition (or series). England also plays such matches in the winter in Commonwealth countries.

Thames, the (geography)
One of Britain's longest rivers (210 miles or 338 km), which flows from south-west England to and through London and into the North Sea. Historically it has been a major trading and communications avenue for London and southern England.

Thames Barrier, the (science and London)
A flood barrier built across the River Thames in central London and opened in 1984, which protects the capital from the threat of flooding. Its gates can be raised as protection and lowered when necessary to allow ships to pass.

Thatcherism (politics)
A general term frequently used to illustrate the political and economic policies associated with Margaret Thatcher, Britain's first woman Prime Minister (1979–90) and leader of the Conservative Party (1975–90). An emphasis was placed on private enterprise, the reduction of public expenditure or government spending, the transfer of state concerns to the private sector, lessening the power of the trade unions and local government, and reducing inflation.

Theft (law)
The legal term to describe the criminal act when an individual takes property belonging to another person with the intention of permanently depriving the other of it.

Theme park (sport and leisure)
A large recreational site, usually in the countryside and privately owned, which illustrates a specific theme or idea like local history, in addition to having other entertainment and leisure facilities. The number of such parks has rapidly increased since the 1980s.

Third reading (government)
The final and usually formal examination of a bill in its passage through the Houses of Parliament, although debate can be demanded at this stage. After the completion of the third reading the bill passes to the sovereign for the Royal Assent.

Third-party insurance (finance)
The obligatory insurance that all motor vehicle drivers must have, which is arranged between two parties (the driver and his or her insurance company). This means that the driver is insured against any damage or injury caused to another person (the third party) in an accident.

Thirty-Nine Articles (of Belief), the (religion)
The list of religious doctrines and beliefs of the Church of England established in 1563 which are generally accepted by all the clergy and members of the Church, and which define the particular characteristics of their denomination.

Three-cornered fight (politics)
A parliamentary or local election which is fought between three political parties, such as the Conservative and Labour Parties and a third party like the SLD or a nationalist party.

Three-line whip (government)
Normally an order paper (in the House of Commons) on which a particular debate or vote is underlined three times by the party whips. This shows that the issue is very important and that party MPs are obliged to attend the debate and the vote. Failure to support the party is regarded as an act of rebellion.

Tied cottage (housing)
A property owned by a particular employer in which the tenant can live only as long as he or she remains in the employment of the employer. This situation is similar to a tied pub, which is owned by a particular brewery and which must purchase liquor only from that brewery.

Tory (politics)
The name of the political party from the seventeenth century to

the 1830s which was the forerunner of the present-day Conservative Party. But the term 'Tory' is still applied to the Conservative Party and its members.

Tote, the (sport and leisure)
The common name for the Horserace Totalisator Board, a state body that organizes and supervises an official betting system for the general public at racecourses throughout Britain.

Tourist Trophy, the (TT) (sport and leisure)
A well known motor-cycle competition (dating from 1907) for motor-cycles of various power classes which takes place on the Isle of Man every year.

Tower blocks (housing)
See **High rise block**.

Town (society)
A large urban settlement which has not been given the status of a city.

Town clerk (government)
The former name for the non-elected leading administrative official of a town council, who served as the town secretary and was responsible for the local bureaucracy. The official is now usually called the chief executive.

Town council (government)
Small towns in Britain may function as limited local government authorities with a restricted number of powers, and are usually part of a larger district or county (regional) council. Larger towns may themselves be a district council or a borough council if they retain the old title. The leading official of such town councils is usually a mayor.

Town hall (government)
A central building in a town or city which has historically contained the offices and administration of local government, and which may still carry on certain limited functions, although it can also serve in some cases as a public hall for concerts and meetings. Such a building in some towns and cities may be called the City Hall or the Council House.

Trade Descriptions Act, the (TDA) (law)
The Act of Parliament 1968 which stipulates that all products and services offered for sale to the public must be accurately described

and not have false or misleading labels. There are criminal penalties for offences under the Act, which is an important part of consumer protection.

Trade gap (commerce and finance)
Also known as the trade deficit where an excess of imports over exports creates problems for the national trade balance, and leads to a deficit or gap. Britain has suffered frequently from this problem in the twentieth century.

Trade Unions, the (TUs) (employment)
Workers' organizations in Britain (of which there are some 323) that campaign for the rights of employees and negotiate with employers on their behalf, as well as providing a range of services for their members. They continue to be influential, although their membership has declined in recent years, and are closely associated with the Labour Party. They vary considerably in size and political beliefs, with the biggest being the left-wing Transport and General Workers' Union with some 1.3 million members, and the second-largest is the Engineers' Union.

Trades Union Congress, the (TUC) (employment)
An umbrella organization, with its headquarters at Congress House in London, which comprises affiliated trade unions (numbering some 80 per cent of all British trade unionists or some 8.4 million people) and was established in 1868 to represent the interests of the trade union movement although the official legalization of trade unions was not achieved until 1871. It campaigns to improve the employment, social and economic conditions of employees, negotiates with government and employers, provides a range of services for its members and holds an annual conference to debate common problems and to decide general policy. Its elected General Council represents the TUC between congresses and implements decisions.

Trafalgar Square (London)
See **New Year's Eve**.

Traffic wardens (transport and law)
Traffic wardens with their distinctive black and yellow-edged uniforms are a common sight in British towns and cities, and are the responsibility of the Chief Constable of a police force area. They control traffic and car parking and issue fines to car owners who are parked illegally. From 1993 traffic wardens in London will be

controlled both by the police and the boroughs, and those in the latter category will be known as parking attendants.

Training and enterprise council (TEC) (employment)
Some 82 TECs have been set up by government in England and Wales in an attempt to promote more effective training at the local level by employers and individuals, and to develop various government training schemes (including education and work experience) such as Youth Training and Employment Training for school-leavers and the unemployed.

Treasury, the (government)
The main state department which is in charge of managing and controlling Britain's national economy and financial policies. The Chancellor of the Exchequer is the senior government minister and member of the Cabinet responsible for the operation of the Treasury.

Treaty of Rome, the (government)
The original 1957 treaty which was signed by six European nations to establish the European Economic Communities, now the European Community (EC). Britain joined the EC in 1973 when the European Communities Act 1972 was passed by Parliament, and was obliged to observe the provisions of the Treaty of Rome. The treaty serves as the basic constitution for the EC.

Trident (military)
The nuclear missile, currently being fitted to four new Royal Navy submarines, which replaces the old Polaris missiles.

Triple Crown, the (sport and leisure)
The title awarded to that national Rugby Union football team of England, Scotland, Wales or Ireland which beats the three other countries in a rugby season.

Trooping the Colour (tradition)
The annual military ceremony on Horse Guards Parade in London, which has been held since the eighteenth century and which now celebrates the Official Birthday of the sovereign (currently in June). Regiments of the Guards Division and the Household Cavalry take part and one regiment is chosen to parade its flag (troop its colour) for inspection before the sovereign.

Troubles, the (politics)
A term for the current violence and sectarian hostilities between

Roman Catholics and Protestants in Northern Ireland which broke out in 1968–9. But it is also used for similar disturbances in Ireland as a whole in the early twentieth century which involved conflicts with the British.

Trust (finance and law)
The legal arrangement whereby control of property is vested by its owner (the settlor) in a trust. Trustees administer the trust for the benefit of a third party (the beneficiary).

Trustee Savings Bank, the (TSB) (finance)
One of the five leading English banks with branches in most towns and cities, providing banking services for private customers and commercial companies. Originally there were many TSBs, which functioned as savings banks, but in 1986 they merged into one bank, the TSB Group, which sold its shares to the public.

Tube, the (transport)
See **Underground**.

Turf, the (sport and leisure)
The term which is commonly used to describe the sport of horse-racing in Britain, presumably deriving from the grass of the race-course.

Turn-out (of voters) (politics)
The number of voters in Britain at a general or local election who actually cast their votes. Turn-out is high for general elections (between 75 and 80 per cent) but much less so for local and European Parliament elections.

Tutor (education)
A teacher in an institution of higher education who may be a personal tutor responsible for the welfare of a certain number of students, or one who teaches and supervises a small group of students. The group sessions are called tutorials.

Tutorial (education)
An arrangement, usually at higher education level, in which students have a weekly meeting with a tutor (teacher) to discuss essays and other work. The ratio may be 1:1 or up to 1:4, with the emphasis being on direct contact between student and teacher.

TV Times, the (media)
An illustrated feature magazine, established in 1968, which contains all the scheduled radio and television programmes for the week on

the BBC and ITC channels. The *Radio Times* does a similar job and competes with *TV Times* in offering this service to the public.

Twickenham (sport and leisure)
The headquarters of the English Rugby Football Union (the sport's governing body) in south-west London. Its well known ground is the venue for the England team's home matches, international matches, and the annual university match between Oxford and Cambridge Universities.

Two-party system, the (politics)
The electoral and political system in Britain which effectively results in governmental power being shared alternately between the two largest parties (the Conservatives and Labour).

U

Ulster (geography)
The ancient kingdom which historically covered the northernmost part of the island of Ireland, and which is now mainly occupied by Northern Ireland (often itself referred to as Ulster).

Ulster Defence Association, the (UDA) (politics)
One of the strongest and largest Protestant paramilitary organizations in Northern Ireland, formed in 1971 as a result of the disturbances in the province, which began in the late 1960s. It has responded to violent actions by the IRA and other extremist Catholic groups, and (since 1992) has been outlawed by the British government because of its terrorist activities.

Ulster Defence Regiment, the (UDR) (military)
A paramilitary part-time reserve force, established by the British government in 1969 but recruited in Northern Ireland. Its role is to take over some of the internal security functions of the British Army and the Royal Ulster Constabulary (RUC). In 1992 it merged with the Royal Irish Rangers to become the Royal Irish Regiment.

(Ulster) Democratic Unionist Party, the (politics)
A political party established in Northern Ireland in 1971 when it separated from the Ulster Unionist Council because of policy disagreements. The party is firmly Protestant, attracts hardline loyalist support, and argues that Northern Ireland should remain an integral part of the United Kingdom (unionist). Currently it has three MPs in the House of Commons and is led by Ian Paisley.

Ulster Popular Unionists, the (politics)
A small, but active, party in Northern Ireland, established in 1980, with one MP in the House of Commons, which supports the union of the United Kingdom.

(Ulster) Unionist Party, (Official), the (politics)
A political party which, as the Ulster Unionist Council, formed the basis of the ruling Protestant Parliament in Northern Ireland from 1921, when Ulster and the Republic of Ireland became separate countries, until direct rule began in 1972. After splits in the Unionist

grouping in 1974 it became known as the Official Unionist Party, and is more moderate than the Democratic Unionists. Most of its supporters are Protestants who wish Northern Ireland to remain part of the United Kingdom. The party currently has nine MPs among the 17 Northern Ireland MPs in the House of Commons.

Undergraduate (education)
A student studying for, but who has not yet passed, a first (usually three-year) degree (BA or BSc) at an institution of higher education in Britain. A postgraduate by contrast is a student who has passed the first degree and is working on a higher degree (MA or PhD).

Underground, the (transport)
An electric railway network which carries passengers through underground tunnels in cities such as Glasgow, Liverpool and London. Construction on the London Underground (commonly known as the Tube) was started in the nineteenth century with the first line opened in 1863. It is now operated by London Regional Transport and carries a system of nine named lines covering 250 miles (404 km) to most areas of Greater London and parts of the surrounding counties, with some 272 stations, and a frequent train service from early morning to midnight.

Underwriter (finance)
A member of an organization (such as an underwriting group at Lloyd's or a merchant bank) that takes financial responsibility for supporting another individual's or body's financial activities or insurance policies, and which is willing to bear any losses which may occur.

Unemployment benefit (finance)
A benefit within the state social security system which is paid to adults who have become unemployed. The benefit lasts for up to 12 months (after which an unemployed person becomes eligible for means-tested Income Support) and the current amount is £43.10 for a single person per week and £69.70 for a married couple. People claiming unemployment benefit have to be available for work if it is offered and are supposed to look actively for work.

Unemployment figures, the (government)
Statistics regarding the number of unemployed people in Britain which are released by the government every month. The unemployed are those members of the labour force who are unable to get jobs for seasonal, technological, economic or educational

reasons. The government has complicated methods of arriving at the unemployment figures, which are often attacked by opposition parties and labour leaders as inaccurate.

Unfair dismissal (employment)
An industrial administrative tribunal will find, when appealed to, that an employee has been unfairly dismissed if the employer has used either an unfair reason for, or procedure in, dismissing that person from a job.

Unfair trading (commerce)
A general term to describe any business practice, such as a monopoly situation, which gives rise to unfair trading, or discrimination between one trader and another. This area is under the control of the government Office of Fair Trading (OFT).

Unified business rate (government and finance)
The money which is raised in the form of a tax on non-domestic properties, such as offices, shops and other commercial buildings, in England and Wales. The rate is set by central government, and collected by local authorities. It is paid into a national pool and then redistributed to local government. In Scotland the rate is levied by local authorities.

Union Flag (Jack), the (tradition)
The formal name of the British national flag, originating from the union of England and Scotland under a single monarch in 1603. It is more commonly known as the Union Jack and now comprises the St George's cross of England, St Andrew's cross of Scotland and St Patrick's cross of Ireland (for Northern Ireland).

Unit trust (finance)
A financial company from which individuals buy a shareholding which is then divided into units. The company invests the money received from the shareholders in a range of other companies. The cost of managing the trust is taken out of the shareholders' income, and the company then distributes any income and profits remaining to the shareholders.

Unitarian (religion)
A religious sect originating in the Reformation period in Europe and developed in England in the seventeenth century. It denies the doctrine of the Trinity, believing that God exists only in one person. Unitarians hold no particular profession of faith, have not adopted

an absolute creed of belief, and are organized democratically in congregations.

Unitary state (government)
The constitutional model which places national or state power in one place or institution in a country, and does not devolve central power to a federal system. The United Kingdom is a unitary state with centralized political and governmental power concentrated on Parliament in London, which legislates for England, Scotland, Wales and Northern Ireland.

United Kingdom, the (UK) (government)
The common abbreviated name for the United Kingdom of Great Britain and Northern Ireland, comprising England, Scotland, Wales and Northern Ireland. It is a constitutional, political or governmental title rather than a geographical one.

United Kingdom Atomic Energy Authority (UKAEA) (science)
A body established in 1954 which was originally concerned with basic forms of nuclear energy, but which is now responsible for Britain's research and development programme in advanced nuclear applications.

United Nations, the (UN) (politics)
An international organization established after the Second World War to maintain international peace and security and to achieve co-operation in solving international economic, social, cultural and humanitarian problems. Britain is a member of its General Assembly and a permanent member of the Security Council, as well as many other UN agencies.

United Reformed Church, the (religion)
A Protestant, non-Anglican church which is one of the Free Churches and has a strong following in Wales. It was created in 1972 by the union of the Presbyterian Church of England and the Congregational Church in England and Wales. Each individual church is independent and decides its own form of service and church administration.

Universities' Central Council on Admissions (UCCA) (education)
A body established by the British universities to provide the central machinery for gathering and evaluating student applications to universities. Candidates list up to five institutions in order of preference, and UCCA circulates the application forms to the appropriate institutions. There is a similar body for polytechnics, the Polytechnics'

Central Admission System, established in 1984. The functions of the two bodies may well be combined in the near future.

University (education)
An institution of higher education, providing undergraduate and postgraduate courses, and carrying out research in many fields. The 47 universities in the United Kingdom had some 334,000 full-time British and overseas students in 1989–90, and numbers have increased considerably since then. Admissions are by selection and are currently administered by the Universities' Central Council on Admissions (UCCA). The universities are independent and are governed by royal charter or by Acts of Parliament, enjoy complete academic freedom, appoint their own staff, and decide which students to admit, which subjects to teach and methods to employ, and which degrees to award. British universities fall into three groups historically: the ancient universities of Oxford and Cambridge and their Scottish counterparts such as St Andrews, Glasgow and Aberdeen; the redbrick universities in large industrial cities such as Leeds, Liverpool and Manchester; and the new universities established since the 1960s such as York, East Anglia and Sussex. The universities, although independent, are funded by public money or taxation given by the government according to student numbers and the quality of research. As more polytechnics achieve university status the number of British university institutions will accordingly rise.

University of Buckingham, the (education)
The University of Buckingham is the only independent or private university in Britain. It was established in stages in the 1970s, provides for a range of undergraduate and postgraduate degrees in the arts and sciences, and awards its bachelor degrees after only two years' study by taking advantage of the whole academic year and cutting down on vacation time.

Unlawful dismissal (employment)
The situation where an employer has dismissed an employee unlawfully by breaching a condition of the worker's contract of employment. The employee may gain substantial damages (money) as a result.

Unofficial strike (employment)
A strike (or stopping of production by employees) which is not formally recognized or initiated by a trade union, sometimes also known as a 'wildcat' strike. Such strikes are not as common as they

used to be, mainly because of unemployment levels and Conservative government legislation in this area.

Unskilled worker (employment)
A worker who does not possess any particular skills, education or qualifications, and who is usually employed in a limited range of manual jobs.

Upper class (society)
The highest social class in Britain such as members of the aristocracy and other people who rank in this class by virtue of their wealth or birth status.

Upper middle class (society)
The middle class ranks socially below the upper class and is usually divided into two, upper and lower. The upper section includes the more wealthy and professional people such as doctors, lawyers, university academics, senior managers, company directors and senior civil servants.

Upper school (education)
The forms or classes in state secondary and independent schools may be divided into a lower and an upper school. The latter consists of the senior classes of the school including the sixth form.

V

Value added tax (VAT) (finance)
An indirect tax levied at a current rate of 17.5 per cent on most goods and services paid for by the customer or consumer, introduced in Britain in 1973, and either included in the price or added to the price at the time of payment. It is not, however, charged on some goods and services such as books, newspapers and magazines, public transport fares, postal services and children's clothes. It is intended that there will be a uniform rate throughout the EC eventually.

Variety (theatre, shows) (arts)
A general term in the theatre and television to describe a mixed light entertainment show, usually with music and different types of acts and artists.

Venture Scouts (sport and leisure)
See **Scout Association**.

Verdict (law)
The decision by magistrates or a jury at the end of a criminal trial, in which they find a person guilty or not guilty.

Vested interests (society)
Those social, political and economic groups in British society which have a particular interest in preserving their own specific roles, status and rewards. Also referred to as interest groups or pressure groups.

Vicar (religion)
An ordained clergyman who serves as the priest in charge of a parish and parish church in the Church of England, and who lives in a vicarage (a church house supplied by the Church Commissioners, usually free of rent).

Vice-Chancellor (VC) (education)
The executive and administrative leader of most universities (and some other institutions of higher education), with overall responsibility for the organization of the institution. He or she may be appointed from within or outside the university and for a period of

years, and may also be known as a Provost, Regent or President. The post of Chancellor of a university, on the other hand, is normally a ceremonial or nominal one given to a public figure, which has few if any executive powers.

Victimization (employment)
A general term, but especially used in employment situations, when a person has lost a job for an unfair reason or has been penalized in some way. It is a form of discrimination, such as the failure to join a trade union in certain circumstances, which may serve as a basis for appeal to a tribunal.

Village (society)
When Britain was a mainly agricultural country (until the early nineteenth century) daily life and activities were centred on the village, which was and is a small collection of buildings and houses, with a relatively small population. The village system still survives, and is thought to represent a quintessentially British (English) way of life in rural surroundings. Villages often have a village green or grass area at the centre of the village and a village hall which serves as a community centre.

Vocation (employment)
Refers to a particular kind of employment, such as the Church and medicine, which is supposed to require a special calling and dedication. It can be used in a looser sense to describe an area of work or any type of job.

Vocational education (education)
The preparation of pupils or students for a specific occupation or range of occupations. It is often distinguished from general or liberal education.

Voluntary organizations (society)
A general term to describe those charitable organizations (of which there are some 170,000 in Britain) that provide voluntary aid, support and services for a wide range of social welfare activities in Britain, such as Help the Aged, Shelter and the People's Dispensary for Sick Animals. They are grouped under an umbrella body, the National Council for Voluntary Organizations (NCVO).

Voluntary school (education)
A state school (primary and secondary) which is maintained or supported by the local education authority (LEA) of a county council in England and Wales, and which therefore receives state

financial aid. Historically they were founded by voluntary or independent bodies, such as the Church of England, the Roman Catholic Church or the Methodists, and are still able to maintain their old denominational identities within the state structure. Some 22 per cent of all students in state schools attend a voluntary school.

Vote, the (politics)
The franchise in Britain, or the right of every eligible person over the age of 18 who is resident in Britain (and some who are absent) to cast a vote in a local or general election.

Vote of censure (government)
A vote taken in government or other organizations which, if passed by a majority, serves as a condemnation of a particular form of action or behaviour.

Vote of no confidence (government)
A vote taken in government or other organizations which, if passed by a majority, states that a body has lost confidence in a leader or party, or a particular form of action or behaviour. In Britain, a government will normally resign if it receives a vote of no confidence in the House of Commons.

Voting system (government)
Voting is not compulsory in the British electoral system whether for local or parliamentary elections. Individual electors register one vote each for their preferred candidate in a secret ballot at a polling station. The candidate who obtains the most votes (a simple majority) wins the election, and there is no proportional representation (PR) system. The same voting system is used for almost all other electoral situations in Britain, both in and outside politics.

W

Wage (employment)
Traditionally the money paid to a worker at the end of the week in return for his or her labour, in contrast to a salary paid monthly. But the term can also be generally used to indicate the amount of money earned by a person whenever paid.

Wage demand (employment)
The claim for more money to be paid to workers, usually made by their trade unions on their behalf.

Waiting list (medicine)
Refers to the time that a patient may have to wait to gain entrance to a hospital or to have surgery. One of the main criticisms of the state National Health Service (NHS), although delays have now been reduced in many hospitals.

Wales (geography)
The country of the United Kingdom which lies to the west of England on mainland Britain, with a population of 2,779,000, and which was united politically with England in 1536. It is a mainly upland country in the north and centre (where Welsh is spoken by some people in northern and western rural areas), with lowland regions around the coasts, where most of the population live and where many of the industrial centres and large towns lie.

Wapping (media)
An area of East London to which many national newspapers have moved from Fleet Street since the 1980s, and where their head-quarters and printing facilities are now situated. Their move was dictated by high rents in central London, and was characterized in some cases (as with *The Times*) by conflicts between newspaper owners and the print trade unions.

Ward (government)
District councils in England, Wales and Scotland are divided into wards (or areas of a town or city) which are used for electoral and administrative purposes. In national elections, each ward will have a polling station at which registered electors vote. In local elections,

each ward will elect councillors from that area to serve on a district council.

Warden (education and society)
The term may be used in many contexts such as the executive and administrative head of hostels, halls of residence, community homes and some colleges of higher education.

Warder (law)
An old term (sometimes still used) to describe prison officers who are in charge of prisoners within a prison.

Warrant (law)
The official document issued by a magistrate which empowers the police in some cases to search a property or arrest a person. It can be a general term to denote the authority to do something, usually of an official nature, and may also be used by banks as payment in financial deals.

Watchdog (government and commerce)
The common name for the independent regulators who oversee the activities of the newly privatized industries in Britain, such as Ofgas, Oftel, Ofwat and Offer.

Water supplies, the (science and commerce)
Water facilities in England and Wales were privatized in 1989 and are now in the private sector. Ten regional water companies are responsible for water supplies, sewage and water treatment, and the charging of costs to the consumer. Water facilities in Scotland and Northern Ireland are currently still in the state or public sector, and are operated by local and central government authorities. The Office of Water Supplies (Ofwat) is the independent regulator monitoring the water companies after privatization.

Weeklies, the (media)
Refers to a wide variety of newspapers and magazines catering for many tastes and interests, which are published on a weekly basis throughout the year such as *The Economist, The New Statesman and Society, Private Eye, Woman, Woman's Own, The Field*, the *New Musical Express*, and influential journals published by *The Times* (*The Times Literary Supplement, The Times Educational Supplement* and *The Times Higher Educational Supplement*).

Welfare state (society)
The term for the range of state programmes which provide for the

health and social welfare of the British population, centring mainly on the social security system, the national social services and the National Health Service (NHS). These cover the basic economic, health and social needs of the people. Sir William Beveridge (1879–1963) was a British economist who produced in 1942 a report which proposed a social security system 'from the cradle to the grave' for all British citizens. Many of his ideas were put into practice by the postwar Labour government (1945–51) as the basis of the welfare state.

Welfare worker (society)
An individual (not necessarily professionally qualified in a specific field) who often works for a voluntary body or charitable organization, which is concerned with providing help and aid to the needy and underprivileged in society.

Wembley (sport and leisure)
The English national sports stadium in North London where the annual FA Cup Final is played. But it also holds a range of other events and international contests such as Rugby League, hockey, speedway racing, greyhound racing, boxing and football/soccer. The 1948 Olympic Games were held at Wembley, and in recent years the stadium has hosted large charity concerts.

Western European Union, the (WEU) (military)
An intergovernmental organization for military, defence and security co-operation, formed in 1955, of which Britain is a member, that has recently been reactivated with the addition of more member-states. It may possibly become the defence and security arm of the European Community (EC), and also take over some of NATO's military functions within Europe.

Westminster (London)
A local government borough in central London (the City of Westminster with its own mayor), which contains the Houses of Parliament, situated in the Gothic structure of the Palace of Westminster, built between 1840 and 1860 to replace ancient buildings destroyed by fire. The term is therefore also used as a short name to describe the central national government.

Westminster Abbey (London and religion)
A large church in Westminster, London, dating possibly from the seventh century, and an important focus of English history. Most

English sovereigns have been crowned in the abbey and it contains memorials to, and the tombs of, distinguished English people.

Westminster Cathedral (London and religion)
The main Roman Catholic cathedral in England, in London, and the seat of the Cardinal Archbishop of Westminster, who is generally regarded as the head of the Roman Catholic Church in England and Wales. It was built between 1895 and 1903, at a time when Roman Catholics had most of their civil and religious freedoms restored.

Whips (government and politics)
MPs in the House of Commons, or peers in the House of Lords, who are chosen by the party leadership to manage the members of their parties in the Houses of Parliament. They encourage active support for the party and its policies, keep party discipline, and make sure that MPs and peers attend meetings and debates and vote (particularly on crucial matters). The Chief Whip, who is normally a senior member of the party, heads the Whips' Office and supervises the other party whips.

White paper (government)
Similar to, but not as widely consultative as, a green paper in Parliament. It is an official white-coloured publication which itemizes the government's policy in a particular matter that will form the basis of later legislation. It will often set out the basics of a draft bill.

White-collar worker (employment)
The term commonly applied to an individual in clerical, office or professional employment, who is distinguished from a manual or blue-collar worker.

Whitehall (government)
The term commonly applied to the government administrative machine, consisting of ministries and departments, which implement the policies of the sitting government. Many of these government buildings are in Whitehall, a street in central London.

Who's Who (society)
An annual reference book, established in 1848, which contains biographical and career information about eminent British (and some non-British) people.

Widow's pension (finance)
The state benefit (currently £54 per week) within the social security

system which is paid to a surviving wife or widow (over 45) after the death of her husband. This payment is frequently incorporated into other benefits such as Income Support.

Will (law)
A legal document expressing the wishes of a person over 18 (the testator) as to the disposition of his or her property after death. In most cases the will must be in writing and witnessed by two people. Distribution of the property of a person dying intestate (without a valid will) is determined by statute.

Wimbledon (sport and leisure)
The headquarters in Wimbledon, south-west London, of the All England Lawn Tennis and Croquet Club, on whose grass courts annual international tennis championships have been held since 1877. Formerly confined to amateurs, they were opened to professionals in 1968. The two weeks of the championships are extensively covered by television and are very much a British institution. The term Wimbledon commonly refers to the tennis championship itself.

Windsor Castle (royalty)
The largest of England's castles, in Windsor, Berkshire, which was built in the eleventh century and is an official residence of the sovereign. Ceremonies, such as the installation of Knights of the Garter, and state functions are held in the castle.

Witness (law)
A person who is called to give evidence on behalf of the defence or the prosecution in a criminal court of law, or by either side in a civil case.

Women's Institute, the (WI) (society)
There are branches of the National Federation of Women's Institutes throughout Britain. It was founded in Canada in 1897, and in 1915 as an essentially rural-based organization in Britain, where it is now the biggest women's voluntary body. It aims to improve the educational, social and cultural lives of women on a national and international basis.

Women's Movement, the (politics)
The term refers generally to the campaign for women's rights and equality with men in Britain. It was used initially to describe the first wave of feminism from the 1860s to the 1920s, which campaigned for women's suffrage (or votes for women). The suffrage

organization founded in 1903 by Emmeline Pankhurst (known as the Women's Social and Political Union) was an important milestone. Its contemporary use refers to the Women's Liberation Movement which started in the late 1960s. In Britain this grew in part from the new left and its student movements, but also from a series of strikes for equal pay from 1968.

Women's Royal Army Corps, the (WRAC) (military)
The former women's section of the British Army, formed originally in 1938. It was disbanded in 1992 and now forms part of the Adjutant-General's Corps of the army. Women operate in many trades and positions alongside men in the army, and can serve in front-line positions in the event of hostilities.

Women's Royal Air Force, the (WRAF) (military)
The women's section of the RAF, originally established in 1918. Women operate in many trades and positions alongside men in the RAF, and can now fly aircraft, not only in transport functions but also in combat roles.

Women's Royal Naval Service, the (WRNS) (military)
The women's branch of the Royal Navy (commonly known as the Wrens), originally established in 1917. Women operate in many trades and positions alongside men in the navy, and are now able to serve in ships at sea.

Women's suffrage (politics)
The right of women to vote. In Britain the campaign started in 1866, but was initially unsuccessful. A limited women's suffrage was granted in 1918 after the First World War, and equal voting rights for all women were achieved in 1928.

Woolsack, the (government)
The large red seat on which the Lord Chancellor sits in the House of Lords when he is supervising the business of the House as its Speaker. It originated in the fourteenth century and is stuffed with wool, representing England's main wealth-creating manufacture and export at that time.

Workers' Educational Association, the (WEA) (education)
A non-sectarian and non-political voluntary body established in 1903 to promote the cause of adult education at a time when working people in particular were becoming better educated and were demanding further educational help and guidance. It now

organizes courses and programmes throughout Britain on a range of subjects at some 900 branches.

Working class (society)
A social class in Britain which is generally regarded as being below middle class and composed of skilled, semi-skilled and unskilled workers.

Working men's clubs (sport and leisure)
Local clubs established in towns and cities throughout Britain which give working-class men the opportunity for relaxation, recreation and meeting each other. They provide a range of games, sports and entertainment.

Work-to-rule (employment)
An industrial protest, similar to a go-slow, but which falls short of an all-out strike. Employees in a factory, office or company closely observe their employment and work regulations, thereby slowing down or decreasing the working patterns and rate of production.

Writ (law)
A legal document in civil law actions requiring the person to whom it is addressed either to do some specific act, or to stop doing something. It may be served by post or by a bailiff on a person or company direct.

Written examinations (education)
The papers that are taken by a pupil or student in order to pass an examination, which is usually three hours long. Used in contrast to an oral examination (where no writing is required), or project work where written work may be completed without the pressure of an examination situation. Written examinations have formed the basis of most of British education.

Y

Young Men's Christian Association, the (YMCA) (religion and society)
A non-denominational Christian body, founded in Britain in 1844 with specifically religious and humanitarian aims. Today it arranges religious, educational and social programmes for young men. It operates regional centres and hostels providing cheap accommodation throughout Britain, and has an international membership (not limited to Christians) of some 10 million.

Young offenders (law)
A general term which can include children from the age of 10 but which usually applies to young people between the ages of 15 and 20 who are convicted of criminal offences and may be given custodial sentences in a young offenders' institution in England and Wales (between 16 and 21 in Scotland and 17 to 21 in Northern Ireland).

Young offenders' institution (law)
A state establishment where young offenders are sent after conviction. The institution provides a custodial punishment, but also aims to give various forms of training which will be useful to the young people on their later release.

Young Women's Christian Association, the (YWCA) (religion and society)
The female counterpart to the YMCA, founded in 1855 in Britain, to provide for the welfare and spiritual development of girls and young women. It operates hostels throughout Britain which provide cheap accommodation for young women, and has an international membership of some 2.5 million.

Youth clubs (sport and leisure)
The many clubs for young people between 14 and 21 throughout Britain which are usually associated with a voluntary body, such as a church or community centre. They provide social, sports and recreational programmes, and may belong to the umbrella national organization, the National Association of Youth Clubs.

Youth court (law)
Children aged between 10 and 17 in England and Wales who are

charged with a criminal offence will be brought before a youth court (formerly called a juvenile court), which will determine their guilt or innocence and punishment. A children's panel in Scotland and a juvenile court in Northern Ireland perform the same function.

Youth Hostels Association, the (YHA) (sport and leisure)
A voluntary organization established in Britain in the 1930s which provides low-cost accommodation in (youth) hostels throughout Britain on a short-stay basis for travellers, such as hikers (walkers) and cyclists, as they visit different parts of the country.

Youth Training (YT) (employment)
A comprehensive state-sponsored scheme to provide all 16-year-old school-leavers with either continuing full-time vocational education to the age of 18, or a period of planned work experience for the same length of time. The scheme was introduced in 1991 and is operated by state-financed training and enterprise councils (TECs) and local enterprise companies (LECs) throughout England, Wales and Scotland.

Abbreviations

AA	Automobile Association
AAA	Amateur Athletics Association
ACAS	Advisory, Conciliation and Arbitration Service
ACGB	Arts Council of Great Britain
AG	Attorney-General
A-level	Advanced Level General Certificate of Education
AONB	Area of outstanding natural beauty
APR	Annual percentage rate
ASA	Advertising Standards Authority
AS-level	Advanced Supplementary Level General Certificate of Education
AV	Authorized Version
BA	Bachelor of Arts
BA	British Academy
BA	British Airways
BA	British Association
BAA	British Airports Authority
BAe	British Aerospace
BAF	British Athletics Federation
BBC	British Broadcasting Corporation
BBFC	British Board of Film Classification
BC	British Coal
BCP	Book of Common Prayer
BE	Bank of England
BEM	British Empire Medal
BFI	British Film Institute
BL	British Library
BM	British Museum
BMA	British Medical Association

BNFL	British Nuclear Fuels
BP	British Petroleum
BR	British Rail
BRNC	Britannia Royal Naval College
BS	British Steel
BSc	Bachelor of Science
BSI	British Standards Institution
B-Sky-B	British Sky Broadcasting
BST	British Summer Time
BT	British Telecom
BTA	British Tourist Authority
BUPA	British United Provident Association
BW/BWB	British Waterways (Board)
CA	Consumers' Association
CAA	Civil Aviation Authority
CAB	Citizens' Advice Bureau
CAP	Common Agricultural Policy
CBI	Confederation of British Industry
CC	Countryside Commission
CC	County Council
CCW	Countryside Council for Wales
CFE	College of Further Education
CGT	Capital Gains Tax
CID	Criminal Investigation Department
CNAA	Council for National Academic Awards
CND	Campaign for Nuclear Disarmament
C of E	Church of England
COI	Central Office of Information
CP	Communist Party
CPS	Crown Prosecution Service
CPVE	Certificate of Pre-Vocational Education
CRE	Commission for Racial Equality
CT	Civic Trust
CTC	City Technology College
CV	Curriculum Vitae
CWS	Co-operative Wholesale Society
DC	District Council
DG (BBC)	Director-General (BBC)
DHA	District Health Authority
DIY	Do-it-yourself
DPP	Director of Public Prosecutions

DVLA	Driver and Vehicle Licensing Agency
EC	European Community
ECHR	European Convention on Human Rights
ECJ	European Court of Justice
EMS	European Monetary System
EMU	Economic and Monetary Union
EOC	Equal Opportunities Commission
ERM	Exchange Rate Mechanism
ESC	English Stage Company
ET	Employment Training
FA	Football Association
FC	Forestry Commission
FCO	Foreign and Commonwealth Office
FE	Further Education
FL	Football League
FT Index	*Financial Times* Index
FT-SE	*Financial Times*-Stock Exchange 100 Index
GB	Great Britain
GCE	General Certificate of Education
GCHQ	Government Communications Headquarters
GCSE	General Certificate of Secondary Education
GLC	Greater London Council
GM	Geological Museum
GMT	Greenwich Mean Time
GNP	Gross National Product
GP	General Practitioner
HC	House of Commons
HE	Higher Education
HEFC	Higher Education Funding Council
HGV	Heavy Goods Vehicle
HL	House of Lords
HM	Her (His) Majesty
HMC	Headmasters' Conference
HMG	Her (His) Majesty's Government
HMIs	Her (His) Majesty's Inspectors of Schools
HMS	Her (His) Majesty's Ship
HMSO	Her (His) Majesty's Stationery Office
HO	Home Office
HP	Hire Purchase
Hymns A and M	Hymns Ancient and Modern

IBA	Independent Broadcasting Authority
ICC	International Cricket Council
ID	Institute of Directors
IHT	Inheritance Tax
ILR	Independent Local Radio
IR	Inland Revenue
IRA	Irish Republican Army
IRN	Independent Radio News
IT	Income Tax
ITC	Independent Television Commission
ITN	Independent Television News
ITV	Independent Television
JC	Jockey Club
JP	Justice of the Peace
KC	King's Counsel
LBC	London Broadcasting Company
LCJ	Lord Chief Justice
LDOS	Lord's Day Observance Society
LEA	Local Education Authority
LEC	Local Enterprise Company
LG	London Gazette
LL	London Library
LM	Lord Mayor
LMS	Local Management of Schools
LP	Lord Provost
LPC	Lord President of the Council
LPO	London Philharmonic Orchestra
LPS	Lord Privy Seal
LR	Lloyd's Register
LRT	London Regional Transport
LS	Law Society
LSO	London Symphony Orchestra
Ltd	(Private) Limited Company
MA	Master of Arts
M and S	Marks and Spencer
Marplan	Market Research Plan
MCC	Marylebone Cricket Club
MEP	Member of the European Parliament
Met	Metropolitan Police
MFH	Master of Foxhounds

MI5/MI6	Military Intelligence Sections 5 and 6
MORI	Market and Opinion Research International
MOT	Ministry of Transport Test
MP	Member of Parliament
MR	Master of the Rolls
MRC	Medical Research Council
MSc	Master of Science
NATO	North Atlantic Treaty Organization
NatWest	National Westminster Bank
NBC	National Bus Company
NCC	National Consumer Council
NCCL	National Council for Civil Liberties
NCP	National Car Parks
NCVO	National Council for Voluntary Organizations
NEC	National Exhibition Centre
NF	National Front
NFT	National Film Theatre
NFU	National Farmers' Union
NG	National Gallery
NHS	National Health Service
NI	National Insurance
NI	Northern Ireland
Nirex	Nuclear Industry Radioactive Waste Disposal Executive
NPG	National Portrait Gallery
NS	National Savings
NSB	National Savings Bank
NT	National Theatre
NT	National Trust
NTS	National Trust for Scotland
NUS	National Union of Students
NYO	National Youth Orchestra
NYT	National Youth Theatre
OAP	Old age pensioner
OBE	Order of the British Empire
OED	*Oxford English Dictionary*
Offer	Office of Electricity Regulations
Ofgas	Office of Gas Supply
Ofsted	Office for Standards in Education
OFT	Office of Fair Trading
Oftel	Office of Telecommunications

Ofwat	Office of Water Supplies
OS	Ordnance Survey
OU	Open University
OU	Oxford University
PA	Press Association
PAYE	Pay As You Earn
PC	Police Constable
PC	Privy Council
PCA	Parliamentary Commissioner for Administration
PCC	Parochial Church Council
PCC	Press Complaints Commission
PF	Procurator-Fiscal
PhD	Doctor of Philosophy
PLA	Port of London Authority
plc	Public Limited Company
PLR	Public Lending Right
PM	Prime Minister
PO	Patent Office
PO	Post Office
PPP	Personal Pension Plan
PPS	Parliamentary Private Secretary
PR	Proportional Representation
PRO	Public Record Office
PSBR	Public Sector Borrowing Requirement
PTA	Parent-Teacher Association
PV	Positive Vetting
QC	Queen's Counsel
Quango	Quasi-autonomous non-governmental organization
RA	Royal Academy (of Arts)
RAC	Royal Automobile Club
RADA	Royal Academy of Dramatic Art
RAF	Royal Air Force
RAM	Royal Academy of Music
R and A	Royal and Ancient Golf Club of St Andrews
RBL	Royal British Legion
RCA	Royal College of Art
RCM	Royal College of Music
RCN	Royal College of Nursing

Rev.	Reverend
RFH	Royal Festival Hall
RHA	Regional Health Authority
Right Rev.	Right Reverend
RL	Rugby League
RM	Royal Mail
RM	Royal Marines
RMA	Royal Military Academy
RN	Royal Navy
RPI	Retail Price Index
RPO	Royal Philharmonic Orchestra
RS	Royal Society
RSA	Royal Society of Arts
RSC	Royal Shakespeare Company
RT	*Radio Times*
RU	Rugby Union
RUC	Royal Ulster Constabulary
RV	Revised Version
SA	Salvation Army
SAS	Special Air Service
SB	Special Branch
SCE	Scottish Certificate of Education
SDLP	Social Democratic and Labour Party
SE	Stock Exchange
SEA	Single European Act
SEAC	School Examination and Assessment Council
SEM	Single European Market
SFO	Serious Fraud Office
SG	Solicitor-General
SIB	Securities and Investment Board
SLD	Social and Liberal Democratic Party
SNP	Scottish National Party
SSP	Statutory Sick Pay
STD	Subscriber Trunk Dialling
TA	Territorial Army
TCP	Town and Country Planning Act 1971
TDA	Trade Descriptions Act
TEC	Training and Enterprise Council
TG	Tate Gallery
TSB	Trustee Savings Bank
TT	Tourist Trophy

TU	Trade Union
TUC	Trades Union Congress
UCCA	Universities' Central Council on Admissions
UDA	Ulster Defence Association
UDR	Ulster Defence Regiment
UK	United Kingdom
UKAEA	United Kingdom Atomic Energy Authority
UN	United Nations
VAT	Value Added Tax
VC	Vice-Chancellor
WEA	Workers' Educational Association
WEU	Western European Union
WI	Women's Institute
WPC	Woman Police Constable
WRAC	Women's Royal Army Corps
WRAF	Women's Royal Air Force
WRNS	Women's Royal Naval Service
YHA	Youth Hostels Association
YMCA	Young Men's Christian Association
YT	Youth Training
YWCA	Young Women's Christian Association